IN
BETWEEN
THESE SHEETS

JAMEEL DAVIS

Cover Designer: Wake Hustle Grind Inc.
Page Designer: Ruth Book Designing
Editor: Idierukevbe Raphael

Publisher: ElevatedWaves Publishing Corp.

ISBN-13: 978-1-7331082-0-1

Library of Congress Control Number:
2019943760

WOW! THAT FELT AMAZING!

Bursting in on amazing,
WHAT? SHE REPLIED!

Ahhhh!
I climaxed to the beat of a heartbeat onto some sheets
that spread so neat.

Gripped the head, stroked the head,
until a long pause marked complete.

Grasped the curves, groped the swerves,
the motions were going to deep,

I rested my hand, stretched my wrist, I picked it back up,
I was almost complete.

My fingers got dry, lubed them back up,
I released my fluids that stained my last sheets.

She told me good luck, they called me back,
congratulations your book is complete.

Cover Model

Hello, my name is Lakia Johnson; born on January 24, 1986 and raised in Cleveland, Ohio. I am a mother of two wonderful boys ages six and fourteen. I am a graduate of East Tech High School, class of 2004. After high school, I attended Cuyahoga Community College (Tri-C) for a short while before transferring to and graduating from Cuyahoga Valley Career Center as a certified Phlebotomist Technician. I am currently employed at University Hospitals Seidman Outpatient Lab.

The medical industry has always been my passion since I was a young girl. What I love most about my position is that it allows me to be a part of team that is saving lives every day. As a Phlebotomist Technician, I collect lab samples from patients seeking medical treatment which is the first step for medical professionals to be able to provide them treatment. With the collection of lab samples, I am able to raise awareness of critical, high and low lab results. I enjoy working with patients and members of the community because I am often able to receive motivation and inspiration to do and become better, as well as be of service to the community by uplifting and inspiring others in return. Working in the medical industry has taught me to be humble and grateful for everything, to eat healthier, exercise and to be happy, because life is too short.

In addition to being a Phlebotomist Technician, I am the Founder and CEO of Beauty On The Go, a mobile Beauty and Spa parlor for young ladies ages 4-12 years old. Beauty On The Go is operated by a glam team that offers Spa parties and Spa days to young ladies in the Cleveland area. We provide manicures, pedicures, facials, makeup, crowns, robes and much more to help young ladies feel like the princess they are during unthemed and themed events such as, birthdays and holidays. It is never too early for young ladies to be mentored, taught self-love, proper hygiene, or to feel inspired. My goal is to inspire young ladies across the world to celebrate their beauty and uniqueness. It is important that our young ladies today learn to value themselves and the skin they are in, so that that can grow to be mature self-loving and respectable women. Beauty On The Go reminds our ladies that their, "beauty begins within."

Outside of being a healthcare professional and business owner, I love nurturing and spending time with my boys who are growing up so fast. I support them in their extracurricular activities, assist them in overcoming adversities and facilitate motivational talks about life. I am a very outgoing, optimistic and adventurist person, who enjoys singing, dancing, trying new things and being in positive atmospheres with optimistic and fun individuals. I was born to stand out, not to blend in. As long as I am alive, my goal every day is to do more than just exist.

Connect with me on Facebook at Beauty On The Go and on Instagram at @BeautyOn_TheGo

In Between
These Sheets

ACKNOWLEDGEMENTS AND DEDICATION

I would like to take this opportunity to thank each and every person that has ever supported my voice. Your investment in me has led to another great publication that is intended for the betterment of you.

"I can teach you the game, but I can't make you play, I can't make you win. You have to play; you have to prepare yourself to win!"

When I was a sophomore or junior at Kent State University, I often read motivational quotes and listened to poets recite their poetry. While reading various quotes and listening to various artists perform live, I often said to myself, "I wish to someday develop the skill to write quotes and to recite poetry in front of large audiences." Today, I am a professional writer, author, speaker and an spoken-word artist.

I used the Law of Attraction to secure my desires; "You are what you think and will become what you believe."

When applying the Law, you have to be mindful of the thoughts you form in your mind and the words that follow out of your mouth because they may stick and become your reality. You have to eliminate your limited self-doubting thoughts, negative words and phrases, negative people, and speak your desires into existence. While speaking the things and the lifestyle you wish to have into existence, you have to work towards your goals using the law of attraction until you reach them.

"I'LL NEVER SELL
MYSELF SHORT
BECAUSE OF THINGS
I'VE BEEN THROUGH,
BECAUSE I COULD BE
PLAYING A KEY ROLE IN
SOMEONE'S LIFE AS I
INSPIRE THEM WITH MY
STORY."

PREFACE

When you read the title, In Between These Sheets, you may have believed in your mind that this is an erotica work. Not quite. Inside these sheets, you will uncover information you can utilize to enhance different areas of the life that you have been provided. Here, you will be inspired to come from in between those sheets of your bed, hit the shower, wash away all toxic energy and prepare yourself to Be Fresh for Greatness. However, you may also be inspired to get back in between your sheets or theirs, and let the sensational vibes created from In Between Her run its course. You can thank me afterwards.

> "A wise man knows he know nothing at all.
> A wise man learns whenever he can, from whoever he can because
> one day he will be glad he did."

During this journey, I found myself getting lost and ending back on the same street. I thought I was too good to pull out a map or ask for help. I had been running out of gas and filling the tank back up thousands of times just to end back on the same street. It's like the neighborhood I was in was one big circle. Being in this neighborhood, brought me down and built me up. This neighborhood stabbed me in the back, spat in my face, and dragged me across the pavement. This neighborhood turned my smiles into frowns, laughs in to cries, and feelings into jokes. However, one day I woke up and told myself I'm ready to leave this neighborhood; so I drove to the Department store to buy a new television set. Walking through the electronics aisle, I saw a GPS (global positioning system) on the shelf which works as a digital map. The saleswoman said it would help me get to locations faster and without getting lost. Being that I was ready to leave this neighborhood, I plugged in my new GPS system and it took me out the circle I was use to driving in. After miles and miles of traveling in circles, after all the potholes I hit, after all the flat tires, and oil leaks, I ended up in this place that was so perfect. I mean this place was beautiful inside out. However, the place didn't accept me into the community just yet. I had to prove that I'm was a great citizen, am loyal, respectful, confident, intelligent, hardworking, caring, and most importantly, I had to prove that I was not here to tear this place apart but to make it better. After tons of effort and hard work, I can finally say I got my foot in the door. This place greeted me by saying, "welcome home, glad to have you a part of our community."

Many of us have built an imaginary fence or gun line in our mind and in our environment, preventing us from obtaining and enjoying a whole cherry pie of our own. Many of us believe that if we cross that imaginary line, we are going to be captured and brought back to the plantation to be punished severely. Although, many of us were brave enough to leave, we still find ourselves looking in our rear view mirror for the bounty hunters; when we have not committed any infraction. The punishment didn't fit the crime, but eventually, we were freed back inside those imaginary fences and gun lines again, withholding us from our true freedom, freedom of self. Only to walk ourselves back inside those concertina wire fences and real gun lines for new crimes committed against our own kind; placing ourselves back in physical chains and in jumpsuits on the very plantation that destroyed us to begin with. Still a SLAVE (Severely Limited At Valuing Education).

Why are many of us trapped inside of our own made up prison, in a cell like a battery (Duracell), draining our energy, without any desire to be recharged, to absorb or shed light?

Is it because we are afraid to change or too lazy to absorb the necessary energy needed to help us outgrow our imaginary caged environment, good energy that will lead us to true freedom, freedom of Self? Or is it because we are suffering from Psychic-Traumatic Slavery

Disorder (PTSD)? A major type of damage or malady to the mind, especially the subconscious mind that occurs as a result of the recurrent distressing experiences of slavery; damage that exceeds one's ability to cope with immediate circumstances, eventually leading to long-term or permanent serious negative consequences.

I believe it is both, more so because of PTSD. I say this because, our entire culture are victims of an ongoing brutal execution of our most prized possession, our mind; which once gave us the capability of building the thriving empires of Egypt, formerly known as Ancient Kemet and which brought African higher learning institutions and flourishing international trade.

Christopher Columbus's conspiracy led to and encouraged the expansion of the African Slave Trade, giving power to slave owners to create caste systems (a division of society based on differences of wealth, inherited rank or privilege, profession, occupation, or race) to keep people of color divided. This allowed European explorers like Christopher Columbus to teach African-Americans and the rest of society that "Africa is a dark continent full of savages" said Sultan A. Latif and Naimah Latif.

Africa is Light, Africa is Rich, Africa is Beautiful, and Africa is the foundation of hue-man kind. People of African descent are amongst the greatest people on the planet. We are all Gods but many of us refuse to and do not know how to activate our true powers. If many of our great people today did not know how great our ancestors were and if they did not learn knowledge of self, they wouldn't have gone on-to do great things. If you do not learn who you are and where you come from, you will never know how to get to your desired destination. Education is essential and powerful, both academic and cultural but it's important that you become a thinker and learn what information is given to you to elevate you and what is given to you to hinder you. Learning who you are and where you come from doesn't start in six grade social studies. In fact, it isn't taught in the American Academic education system at all. Learning who we are and where we come from should be taught by anyone who takes on the role of education; our parents, ancestors, community leaders, athletes, music and television stars. Only a small amount of those people have taken on the tasks, while many others are catering to the oppressors plans of destroying people for monetary items and fame.

Have you ever wondered why your first teachers, whom are your parents as well as traditional educational and spiritual institutions, have never taught you about you, but have taught you about everyone else, their history, thoughts, ideas, inventions and successes. Have you?

At this very moment, forget everything anyone has ever taught you about you, your supreme being, energy, life, the universe, love, education, and the American dream. Strip your mind and spirit naked of all that you think you know and the social influencers who have shaped your perception of reality and have never presented you with the GPS coordinates that lead you to finding the real you. Empty your glass; it's time you be filled with a plethora of knowledge that will work to help free you from your own prison, opening up your internal and external gates. Those that we and the world have shut. Learning our true knowledge of self is vital for escaping mental captivity and achieving greatness, because it's when we see ourselves in our own light, that we go on to create masterpieces and inspire our very own people to do the same. Having control of your thinking allows you to have control of your future.

Now dive IN BETWEEN THESE SHEETS and I'll see you at the other end.

WARNING

THESE SHEETS HAVE BEEN
SECRETED ON WITH FLUIDS
ERUPTED FROM THE PINEAL
GLAND THAT HAVE LED
HUE-MANS TO EXTREME
ECSTASY.

PROCEED WITH CAUTION

Life is all about understanding, changing and adapting.

If you spend your valuable time trying to patch up every scratch, you won't ever be able to enjoy the moment and the journey ahead.

Something's, we just have to handle, let go and move forward from. Neither of us will ever have a problem free path. Life is not designed that way.

It's not the problems and issues that prevent us from succeeding, but the way we react and respond to them.

Many of us desire stability and consistency in our personal lives; career, family, relationships, etc. When I think of stability, I think of a building. Buildings stay put for many years and are resistant to change.

So, for me, a person who wants stability doesn't desire to grow or change. Those who are stable will soon sustain wear and tear, and damages which will be too expensive to repair.

When I think of being consistent or requiring someone to be consistent with me, it's like a machine stamping the same logo, the same way, on the same kind of envelope over and over again. Most people do and require others to do the same thing over and over, while expecting something different. That's the definition of insanity.

You or that person cannot and will not grow that way.
In this life, you have to be comfortable with change because you were created to be a limitless, loving and flexible being. I am not saying it will be easy, but after you have learned to understand, change and adapt, I promise it will be all worth it.

01

AMELIORATE
YOUR MIND

"It's not that you haven't been taught, you didn't have the desire to learn."

ABSENT KNOWLEDGE OF SELF MEANS YOU DO NOT EXIST

-- Jameel Davis PROVERB

One day you will learn to love you for the person our creator have created you to be, so that you too may shine in the horizon.

"Self-Love is the key to making your dreams manifest."

Once you are able to see yourself in the brightest light, you will become more powerful.

I cannot show you how to love you because I am not you. That is something you have to teach yourself.

When you do, you will become that butterfly in the horizon flying free for all of the world to see.

FAITH WITHOUT WORK IS DEAD

Don't tell me you lost hope
and gave up on your dreams?

Right when you gave up,
that's when your dreams were
getting ready to unfold.

All you needed was one more big push.

Now you have pushed your
dreams back another six months,
maybe a year or longer.

Most successful people will tell
you, right before they gave up,
the rewards and blessings came.

We wanted to quit so badly because
people weren't supporting us and we
weren't getting anywhere.

But there's one thing we all had in
common and that one thing got us
to where we are now. **That one thing
is belief.**

Regardless of who was against us and
who didn't support us, we believed in
ourselves that we will make it and we made
it with effort.

So, when you feel like giving up, push a little
harder and believe a little stronger.

Have Faith and you will succeed.

I could almost guarantee that,
**if you invest the same amount
of time, if not more, on enhancing
your mind** as you do your physical
appearance, you'd be in a better place
mentally, emotionally, spiritually,
financially and physically.

If you are only doing what you are doing
because other people are doing it
and because other people love it,
you are doing it for the wrong reasons.

Do what you do because it's true for you to do,
not because everyone is doing it or because other
people approve of it.

When You Deploy Your Internal Rocket,
Greatness Explodes!

How will we ever grow, if we don't fail?

We have to fail forward in order to become better. So, there's nothing wrong with you taking the wrong path as long as you end up back on the right path.

Don't beat yourself up for not being where you wanna be right now, because right now may not be the right time and right now isn't your final destination.

The process is hard, which it is supposed to be given the cards we are dealt. But, it will all be worth it when you finally stand on the horizon and see how far you have come.

I learned along the way. I am still learning and failing forward.

Continue to Wake Hustle and Grind toward reaching the next level.

The difference between me and most people is,
when the pressure got heavy, I continued to fight back
while others allow it to consume them.

Greatness really doesn't come to those who don't have that
burning desire inside to win, despite the obstacles that are in the way.

**If you don't have that ' Willpower" to go that extra mile,
to read an extra chapter, to wake up an extra hour earlier,
to open closed doors, to step outside the norm, to push through
hate, prejudice, tough times and or criticism, you won't ever get
to become great.**

You may become great at failing, but not great at being the best you.
Rewards don't gravitate to those who give up on themselves.

"When Life Knock You Down, You Get Your Butt Back Up and Fight
Back."
If I were to push you down, you'd jump up in a heartbeat to fight me
back.

Use the momentum you would use to fight me or anyone else to push life
back and get what you deserve.

Eventually, the wall will give in and you will breakthrough.

This is how roses make their way through cement.

BUILD FROM WITHIN

You have such a beautiful frame, but
it's your mind that is holding you back
from creating a beautiful legacy.

Your mind is in need of a complete
renovation. **Cleanse your mind**, body
and spirit and you will become a masterpiece.

If you do not think highly of yourself or feel great about yourself, you aren't able to receive the love others are giving you because you do not have love for yourself. In fact, you aren't able to achieve your desires and operate at your fullest potential.

Because you do not see yourself in the highest light, do not feel complete within, and because you are not able to recognize and receive the love someone is giving you, your personal insecurities, self-doubt, and low self-esteem serves as a deterrent to the love and blessings that are trying to come your way. You are pushing it all away.

You cannot expect anyone to love you or mention they do not love you, or expect to receive blessings if you do not know what love look or feel like. You should not be dating or be involved with anyone until you see yourself in the highest light and feel great about your entire being because you are going to run a good person away by beating on yourself.

If you are expecting someone to fill a void that only you can fill, they are going to fall short every time which will cause you to become upset and angry, driving them away.

Take time out to learn you. Spend time alone ignoring the voices of your parents, of the community, of the establishment and embrace who you were created to be. Practice speaking highly of yourself, hugging yourself, dancing with yourself, singing to yourself, challenging yourself and going on adventures by yourself. This is how you will develop love of self, receive your desires and how you will be able to recognize and receive love from others.

WHAT WILL YOUR OBITUARY READ?

I've read some with only two sentences.

Your life has a timeline: what matters is what you
do with your life from the time you are born until
the time you pass away.

What will you be remembered for?

Someone who violated the rights of other human beings?

Someone who had aspirations but didn't have the drive to see
things through, or someone who lived a positive life, achieved
everything they desired and gave back to those in need?

Choose to fill your gap with nothing, and people will remember you as
nothing.

WHO ARE YOU?

If someone were to ask, "Who are you?" What would be your initial response? Would you tell them who you are or would you just tell them your name?

If you respond by giving your name, the answer to that question would be incorrect. If the person presented the question, what is your name? You would have answered correctly.

Who are you and what is your name are two different questions and it's important that you answer each one correctly and with confidence.

Everyone wants to feel a sense of purpose, a sense of belonging, to feel accepted by others and to be recognized for whom they are and what they have accomplished. However, when many are given the space to share themselves with others, they become voiceless, as if they do not exist. They know their name, but nothing else about themselves. In addition, many do not know the true meaning behind the name their parents have given them.

Having no understanding of who you are; no identity of your own, opens you up to be defined and controlled by others.

So, when you are asked, who are you? You are invited to share with the person a summary of who you are. If you know who you are, tell them. They may be the person holding the key to your destiny. If you do not know who you are, allow me to share with you why it's important for you to understand who you are.

Picture yourself waking up in a room; a dark room with a litted candle sitting in the corner. You walked over to where the candle is sitting and picked it up so you can figure out where you are. As you begin to turn, you begin to see obituaries fill the walls; obituaries of people who look just like you. After peeking inside a few of those obituaries, you noticed many of them had only a few sentences in them, describing the deceased person.

"De'Shaun Maurice Williams was born on July 21, 1998 to Desiree Johnson and Duron Williams. De'Shaun attended Philadelphia City Schools, where he played football and basketball. He loved Jordan Tennis shoes, hanging out with his friends and sharing laughs with his family. De'Shaun left behind his sister, Tatiana; his brother, Tayvaughn, his mother and father, and a host of friends and loved ones who loved him dearly."

After reading, you begin thinking to yourself, what if this was me on the wall? What would they write about me? Would I mean anything to anyone? What legacy would I leave? Will I die with unachieved goals or dreams? Do I still have time to correct my behavior and attitude toward others? Can I still achieve goals and help others achieve theirs?

While moving along, scanning the walls, you bump into a large object near the center of the room that you weren't aware of before and jumped with fear to what appeared to be the sound of a trunk closing. When you turned and faced it, you noticed it was a coffin you had bumped into. Uncontrollably scared and nervous, your mind begins to race about who could possibly be inside this coffin. Who did I lock in there?After a few minutes have gone by, you decide to approach the coffin and open it. With your head turned away and your heart racing, you gradually open the coffin with your hand until it opened. As your heart begins to pound harder as if it was going to explode out of your chest, you slowly start turning your head back to look inside. When you turned to face the coffin, you noticed someone there in the coffin. YOU! Then the lights turn on.

QUESTIONS TO CONSIDER:

WHO ARE YOU?

Do you know your deepest thoughts, desires and emotions? What about your character traits, your values, what makes you happy, and why you think and do the things you think and do?

Do you know how to separate who you are and what you want to be from what the world thinks and wants you to be?
Are you a dead man/woman walking? Or are you living out your true purpose?
Is your obituary going to be filled with great accomplishments and will your funeral be filled with loving people who will carry your name on?

ACCEPT THE CHALLENGE TO "CULTIVATE YOUR MIND TO OWN THYSELF."

Birthed with the intentions of helping men and women discover their purpose and take ownership of their lives, "Cultivating Minds To Own Thyself "is a book that encourages readers to define, identify and to accept themselves without using society's standards. It teaches readers how to examine themselves in attempt to modify their thoughts and in turn become their best self and make a difference in the lives of others.

AVAILABLE EVERYWHERE BOOKS ARE SOLD

You need you more than
You need anyone else!

So, find you before finding someone
worth you being with, because when
that person Find Out That You Are A
Lost Soul, **They Will Be M.I.A. Too.**

BE YOURSELF

The best thing you can be in life is,
"YOU."

It's much difficult to follow and to fit in.
It requires too much time, effort and dedication.

Time wasted on following the crowd and
trying to be accepted by those who do not
matter, could be invested in you, and getting you
to where you want to be in life.

Those whom you are trying to impress,
only want you where they can reach you,
close enough to bring you down whenever
they feel the need to.

You deserve to be higher, unreachable to those
who are not worthy of your time.

WORDS STICK

Be mindful of the words you use
when talking about you and because
they may stick and **become your reality.**

DON'T CHANGE WHO
YOU WERE CREATED TO BE

Beauty lies within, not just on the surface
of your skin.

You can't allow anyone to identify who
you are, especially those on social media.

Our Creator made you perfect in its image
and likeness. So, why change what was created?

Until you understand that, **until you fill your
interior with self-love,** with the spirit of
the creator, you will always struggle with who
you are.

MISTAKES

Mistakes are common,
they shape us into who we
are **and who we will become.**

There's a reason why
there's an eraser on
the back of a pencil.

KNOW YOUR WORTH

Whatever you advertise is what consumers are out to get.

For example, if all you show to the world is sexually suggestive pictures of you, but talk about you wanting a good man or woman, all that your consumers are going to want is your body.

If you advertise money, cars, clothes, jewelry etc. your consumers are only going to want what they see.

Good men and women don't want what every individual have access to, they only want what can be shared with them.

Sexually suggestive images that reveal mostly buttocks, breasts and other private areas **show that all you have to offer is good sex, nothing more.**

So, you will mainly attract individuals who are only seeking sex.

If a television commercial advertises the new iPhone, people who are only interested in the device, but not the full benefits of the company will be in the checkout line. They want it so they can say they got it, and once it gets old, they are onto something new.

The same thing goes for you.
Know your worth!

WHAT'S THE POINT OF DOING SOMETHING, IF YOU DON'T HAVE CONFIDENCE THAT YOU CAN DO IT?

If you say you can't do something,
and try to do what you said you can't
do, guess what?

You Don't Succeed.

Reassure yourself that you can do
it, even if you get it wrong the first few
times.

**Get back up and try again with the same
faith you started with.**

Eventually, that task will get accomplished.

CONFIDENCE

Have confidence in all that you do, even
if the outcome doesn't work out as you
had planned.

Confidence in your mistakes and
failures result in success. Extreme failures
come to those who don't believe in themselves.

**Try not to worry about things or situations
that are beyond your control.** Worry is harmful
and it causes indecision. An undecided mind
may lead to an undecided heart, and an undecided
heart may lead to a form of action that you may
not be able to fix.

Clear your mind of worries. Worries can kill you
faster than a bullet. Feed your mind with positive
thoughts. Positive thoughts create a positive and healthy heart
and a positive healthy heart creates a successful outcome.
Especially if you believe in yourself.

HOW LONG WILL I REMAIN A WORK IN PROGRESS? WILL I EVER REACH MY MARK? WILL I DIE INCOMPLETE?

Maybe you are already perfect.
Maybe you are allowing the limiting thoughts of others
and the self-doubting thoughts of yours to prevent
you from exploring your real value and seeing the complete you.

You are perfect. Reason being, every experience of yours is unique and created especially for you.

Only you can experience those experiences the way you have and are experiencing them.

Every cell, piece of tissue, organ, bone and system in your body was created perfectly for you. You are perfect because you are you and no one can become you. Your failures, mistakes, pain, successes and moments of happiness are perfectly made just for you.

You are not anyone else, and that's the beauty of being perfect; the beauty of being you.
So, be perfect in all that you do, your highs and lows. No one in the world is you, you are perfectly created.

However, you can always improve your perfectness.

EVERYONE IS ALWAYS WATCHING.

Even those with the power to
get you to your desired destination.

But if you are carrying yourself
unpleasantly, **those onlookers will
not invest in you.**

I refuse to carry myself less than a
responsible and respectful man should.
Opportunities come often and I don't
want to miss my next flight.

Don't miss out on your next opportunity
because you behave inappropriately.

The more you spend on negativity,
The **less you spend** on positive things
for yourself and your family.

SO WHAT IF PEOPLE HATE ON YOU!

The fact that you have to acknowledge that people are,
shows that you are controlled by them.

What benefit do you get by thinking and acting based on what others
think or say about you?

So what if someone is jealous or envious of you,
ignore them and vibrate on a higher frequency.

#ElevateYourWaves

You don't get rewards because you have haters.
You do lose value by entertaining those who think less of you.

When someone hurts your feelings,
you don't have to retaliate by airing their faults, personal business
or make lies about them to the world to get even or attention.

Either you fix the problem with proper conflict resolution or **ignore them
and let it go.**

All that energy invested in trying to get even is destroying the good in you,
and that energy could be invested in getting you where you want and need
to be.

If a man and or a woman carries him/herself less than a man/woman should, instead of degrading them and blasting their wrong doings all over social media and all over the world, take the opportunity to help them correct their wrong doings.

Help them blossom into that successful and loving adult they have the potential to be. Their parents may have not been in the picture or may not have been knowledgeable enough to teach them how to act like a man or lady. Since they were never taught, they may never know.

"Help our sisters develop nurturing relationships and to walk with great character. Helping her helps you become a greater you."

"Help our men develop into loving and responsible men so they can take care of their families and communities."

The Elevator has to be at the bottom
before you are able to reach the top
floor.

Instead of criticizing people for not
being on your level, how about you
send the elevator back down and help
them up!

**- You haven't gotten to where you are
without assistance and resources, so,
don't fault anyone else for being in the
same position you were once in.**

Stop forcing your Hustle and Dreams on everyone else and belittling those who choose to, or who are forced to live differently.

Everyone can't be rich, be business owners, home owners, travel the world, have amazing credit scores and so forth. That is not how the world is designed to be

Stop faulting people for not walking in your shoes and down the same path you walked. They were created differently for a reason, they have a different shoe size and wear different shoes for a reason; and that's to walk their own path that was designed specially for them.

If they desire to walk your path, they will reach out to you for your GPS coordinates.

Until then, value the life they have chosen to live and if you are unable to help those who are controlled by systematic oppression, including systematic discrimination and racism, just do us all a favor and silence yourself.

When most people are seriously hurt,
they hide so you can't see them.

In hiding, everyone becomes a target,
especially those who they feel they
have to retaliate against because of the pain.

They will try and do anything to keep you from
seeing the pain that has been inflicted.

But you can recognize the pain **based on how
they treat other people.** They will make jokes
about others lack and bad circumstances. Some
may even rob and kill as a result.

For those of you who are in hiding because of your pain, understand this; you aren't alone and you don't have to experience the pain much longer. Definitely, not by yourself. But, it starts with self if you really want to heal.

Recognize within yourself that you are hurt and the pain is unbearable. Affirm that you do want better and wish to feel complete. **Next, remove yourself from unwanted energy that makes you feel unease, music, people, television and certain environments.** Then go to a happy place, bring a journal and pen with you. Once you have arrived, breathe and begin writing, from the beginning, the start of your pain and unhappiness. Let it all out. Write how things could have been better. In your writing, express forgiveness to those who've harmed you and apologize to those whom you have harmed because of the pain you have endure.

Now, write out a detailed plan of your goals and dreams and how you wish to get there. Be specific about the kind of life you desire. Once you are finish, share your journal with the world because in order to heal, you must reveal. You will then realize that you were never alone and that people share similar experiences. What happens next is that you get to receive true love, compassion and respect from many others, which will allow you to grow into the person you wish to become. You will be free from the pain.

Finally, go home and work on becoming that person you wish to become. Whenever you are feeling down, go back to that happy place and start writing again. Repeat the process.

ICEBERG IMAGE

Ben Nobbs stated in his presentation of "The Iceberg," that, only 10% of an iceberg is visible.

The remaining 90% is below sea level. How much we can see of an iceberg is the exact same of what we can see in other people.

Majority of people only reveal 10% of who they are, who they are pretending to be, which is their fake image. The other 90% is hidden under the waterline. They create this 10% image for the world to see because they are afraid of being hurt, judged, laughed at or criticized.

Some pretend to be happy, rich, tough, that perfect husband, wife, pastor, teacher, doctor, lawyer, nurse, rapper, model, etc., for society to see. They advertise their money, jewelry, clothes, houses, cars, electronics, hotel rooms etc., but they hide their true being; their feelings behind a still photograph, a video clip, a television screen and behind a Facebook or Twitter post. They hide the fact that they are struggling with something, neglecting their children, their bills are up to the roof, they can't make rent this month, they are depressed, angry, frustrated, are very ill or have made a poor decision.

It's when you reveal the 90% that you get to experience the joys of life, true love, compassion, intimacy and respect. In order to heal, you must reveal.

I reveal my 90% often, because I'm living a human experience just like you, and problems occur and schedules change. But it's when I reveal my deepest feelings that I experience true love, respect, kindness, compassion, and am able to experience the joys of life.

I reveal my emotions in many ways, by sharing them with my confidants, fellowshipping, writing and poetry, which I share publicly because I'm not influenced by what the society thinks. If I allow others to define me or my work, I wouldn't be me, I'd be the society.

A clouded mind is harmful. That's when stress starts to build up and you begin to lose focus and begin to self-destruct. The goal is to keep it cleansed so you can allow great thoughts and ideas in. How do you cleanse it? By revealing the true emotions in it. Reveal them to someone. If you have no one to reveal it to, write it down and throw it away, or write a song or poem. Whatever you do, get it out of your mind so you can be free to be yourself.

YOUR CHILD (REN) OR ANYONE ELSE SHOULD NOT HAVE TO PAY FOR THE PAIN YOU'VE ENDURED IN YOUR PREVIOUS RELATIONSHIPS, ESPECIALLY WHEN THEY PLAYED NO PART IN IT, LOVE YOU AND HAVE TRIED TO HELP YOU.

Heal Yourself, Love Yourself,
Forgive Your Abuser(s), Love Your Child (ren) and Others in Return.

Failure to do so will result in self-destruction and your child (ren), persons of interest, and loved ones skipping out on you.

Express Yourself Fully

Many folks are afraid of what people
will think and say of them, so they hide
their true gifts, talents and opinions.

Those people are not your creator.
They don't have the power to do
nothing, except run their minds,
mouths and fingers.

Those who fix their mouths to
say something negative about what
you express for yourself, **are already
drowning in their own sorrow and
misery.**

Because they aren't capable of rising,
they want you to experience discomfort
just as they are.

Part of being an adult is full self-
expression, rather than people liking you
or not.

Become the best version of yourself
and express yourself fully.

It's your life, not theirs.
So own it!

BALANCE

In order to live a great life, you must balance,
time, health, money and relationships.

Investing too much time in making money puts
your health and relationships with others at risk.

When you invest too much of your time with others,
you lose out on money and maintaining your health.

When you focus too much on your health, you miss
out on money and time with those who matter most.

**Too much time invested in one area, causes you to lose out
on all other areas. You must work to balance them all.**

Me: I use the least amount of time, effort, and energy,
to make the most amount of money, so my health isn't
at risk, and so that I can spend time with those who
matter the most.

PROTECT YOUR MOST VALUABLE ASSET, "TIME"

There are people who will attempt to milk your time to benefit themselves, and who will not acknowledge or invest in your responsibilities.

Usually, these kinds of folks have minimum duties in life; some have everything handed to them and some leech off others to get by. Either way, they are blinded by what you stand for.

When you are faced with such individuals, consider them void because **selfishness is a negative tendency** and it is harmful to your existence.

Don't risk losing everything you have for someone who isn't adding value to your purpose and existence. Manage your time effectively. Every window you get doesn't have to be filled with the presence of certain individuals, fill it with whatever you choose.

We slow down so those traveling behind us won't get lost. But what happens when you take the next exit to the right and they still miss it?

You have to wait another 5, 10, 15 minutes for them to get off, go around, get back on and get off on the right exit.

Now, you are late to your big meeting, vacation destination, etc., missing out on key minutes/moments. This doesn't happen just once, but over and over with multiple people.

Add up the time lost, money spent **and other resources wasted waiting on those who didn't value your time,** patience, worth, profession, family, etc. That's how much time that could have been invested in pushing forward and helping those who were already at the edge waiting to jump. Those who weren't ready to jump, mostly likely won't compensate you for your time, money and efforts. So be mindful of people who may jeopardize what you have going on with their tardiness, lack of resources and willpower.

Focus Less Time and Resources On Those Who Aren't Capable Of Getting You to the Next Level.

There was a time where we were able to recycle waste, making new things out of it. However, time was never one of them. You just can't recycle time.

Today, we go through resources so quickly without the thought of sustainability. We can't recycle most of what we have already used.

This year and every year forward, **we shall make it our duty to spend less of our time and resources on those who aren't ready to rise and those who aren't grateful to us and who can't help us secure our desires.**

Our extra time and resources could be used to secure dreams they would have prevented us from achieving.

It's time for them to rise up, and it's time for us to manage our time and resources effectively.

WHO ARE MY FRIENDS?

Your friends aren't the ones who think highly of you 24/7, who only compliment you when you are doing your best, who are only around when you are looking your best. They are there at your worst and help carry some of your load for you.

Anyone not uplifting you and encouraging you to be your best is not your friend. Anyone who encourages you to use dangerous drugs and consume alcohol regularly, as well as influence you to engage in criminal activity has no respect for you.

If they had respect for you, they would have respect for themselves. If they had respect for themselves, they wouldn't settle for something as low as drug and alcohol abuse, and criminal behavior.

Anyone who encourages you to spend your time and money carelessly on things that have no value aren't your friends.

Your real friends make your problems theirs and work alongside of you to create solutions. They don't just send up a prayer and tell you everything will be alright. Your true friends will put in their best efforts to ensure that you become the successful individual you are destined to be.

When you make the proper adjustments in your life
such as shaking off unwelcome energy and people,
things will start falling into place for you.

But right now, **you are comfortable with being uncomfortable
with unwelcomed people** who are leaching onto you with
unwelcomed and toxic energy.

GETTING TO YOUR DESIRED DESTINATION

It's when you have fought
through the turbulence,
that you are able to cruise
at your desired altitude.

Once at this state, anchor
your mind to the many
spiritual beings that have
created an atmosphere
filled with peace, love, joy,
relaxation and happiness.

Allow these beautiful spirits to
feed your subconscious mind
and soul so you can arrive joyously
at your desired destination.

I believe when you ask your higher power for something,
you are really speaking to the spirit within yourself, **because
it is you who decides whether or not to put in the effort to achieve
what it is you are asking for.**

*When I speak into me, I achieve what it is I desire. I don't call on
anyone but me. That's how I got to where I am today.*

The same people who didn't support your dreams and desires, will be the same people with their hand out when you make it to your desired destination.

What will you do at that point?
Feed that hand or give them a high five?

REFLECTION IS PART OF GROWTH

We are often in GO mode,
in a hurry with our plans
and very seldom sit and reflect
on our life.

**Take a moment and reflect back
to where you are coming from,** all that
you have endured, even the good,
and look ahead to where you want
to go.

The same faith and effort that
got you to your good times and
through bad times will get you
to your desired destination.

Reflection allows you to see how
far you've come and it allows you
to go where you are headed next.

Never Give Up and Never Lose
Focus. Keep Pushing!

LIFE IS ALL ABOUT GROWTH
- Don't Dwell Cn The Past, You Will Be Stuck There.

WOMEN HAVE NO RIGHT TO MESS WITH A MAN THAT SHE KNOWS HAVE A WOMAN!

I have been meaning to tackle this particular discussion for some time now and after seeing a tweet on twitter one morning, I was encouraged to speak on it briefly.

"Ladies I understand the ratio to men to women is something like 10:1. However, that doesn't give you the right to mess with a guy & you "KNOW" for a fact he has a lady.... IT'S LAME"

Because I am a writer, the sentence should read, the ratio of men to women is something like 1:10. There's a famous saying that says,
"there's someone for everyone."

The truth is, there is someone for everyone, but they may not have that person all to themselves. Women in particular; especially black women. I say this to say, for every black man, there is about twenty or so black women. Out of the few black men we have, many make up the jail and prison population and are preparing for their home on the inside for crimes against humanity and the justice system many say is corrupt. Many are filling up cemeteries, dying in the hands of our own kind or by justifiable homicides caused by white uniformed officers.

Out of the men who are buried, caged, and who are preparing for entry or reentry, the ones we have left are ones who are either great and are already with a woman and/or a family, are great but are apart of the LBGTQIA community, are great and single but are working on their dreams, businesses and careers, and those who are walking vegetables and who are destroying the light within our women.

Many people I've spoken to over the years didn't believe me when I said, "monogamy in the black community/culture is going to reach a dead end..."

So what's a black girl or woman who is heterosexual and cultural-oriented to do?

- Love herself and herself only for the rest of her life?
- Birth her own babies she's been longing to have?
- Marry her?
- Wait patiently for a brother who is never coming home?
- Wait to Marry a deceased man in the afterlife if there is one?
- Become a mistress?
- Join the LBGTIA community?

You tell me.

I suggest she do what's best for her and not what the world suggests for her to do. And because the ratio of black men and black women doesn't match up evenly, I personally cannot disagree with, or belittle a black woman for trying to fill a void within her, a void that every woman is trying to fill that is caused by both social engineering and propaganda that is beyond her control. The writer of the tweet says, it's not right for a woman to be involved with a guy that she knows already has a woman because it's lame. Being a lame built our civilization and our culture. So, if being a lame makes you feel secure due to circumstances that are beyond your control, then be a lame. Especially, if it is for the forward advancement of our culture and your happiness.

The Ratio of men to women is 1:20, so what happens when all black men are gone and there are only women? How will our culture advance?

"Mission is Greater than Self and Self shouldn't be selfish. Limited thoughts that are only in favor of your personal desires and not the betterment and advancement of our culture is harmful to our existence."

Don't let them stop you from evolving.
Let us see your wings.
Fly!

Prom is over.

You have graduated from High School.

You have secured that job.

You have finished college.

You have started a family of your own.

You have financed your car and home.

You have married the man or woman of your dreams.

After achieving those goals you have set for yourself, now what?

Success has no end point, **the sky is not the limit, there's no ceiling.** The moon has been walked on.

YOUR GROWTH IS **LIMITLESS.**

He brought her out of her hideout.
He encouraged her to spread her wings.
He accepted her for who she was.
He didn't care if she was a bad chick or not, or if she had it all.
All he wanted to do is ease her from all the pain and hurt that was done in the past.
He wanted to put those missing pieces of her puzzle back together.
He actually is the missing piece of her puzzle that she needs.

He is, Cleveland Author, Jameel Davis.

02

HER

FRIEND-ZONE

Even when I knew he wasn't right for you in whom I said nothing to you about
as your friend when you pushed me away to reap all of his temporary forever's in a matter of weeks or months, I maintained true to my being.

I have never fixed my lips to disrespect you, deceive you, to kiss you, nor to request sexual advances.

But I have fixed my lips to speak highly of you, to honor you, to uplift and to inspire you.

I have never and will never fix my hands and arms to harm you, but I did fix them to hold you, love you, support you and to protect you.

All I ever wanted was to be your friend and nothing more.
But you ended our growing friendship for a guy who only wanted several nights with you and nothing more.

Oh, and the girl next door.

Remember I taught you how to spot those kinds to avoid being hurt?

Wait, you didn't take notes, and as a result you became blinded by his first words.He is no longer present and now you feel as if your heart and spirit is shattered to pieces. And now, you are reaching back out to me to help you pick up the pieces.

"Good Morning, Good Afternoon, Good Night, How Have You Been?"

Nothing!

"Who is Jameel? Oh he's nobody!"

Now it's, "Hey Best-Friend."

Where were you when I needed my friend? Oh that's right, In Between His Sheets and pants.

Hey, you want to meet up for lunch or stop by for dinner? We can talk about it then.

After a couple of bites and noticing that I am still the same man but slightly different, you pull at my drawstring trying to get a taste and feel of my member.

Friend-Zone! Friend-Zone! Friend-Zone!

Remember?

Passionate thrusts of this precious magical wand of mine would only be a temporary fix to your pain.

You would be blinded again mistaking me for what's his name?

Our friendship was never built this way, and it sure isn't about to begin today.

Remember, all I ever wanted to be was your friend and you pushed me away.

I came by to tell you how I feel and to let you know that things will be ok, and the love I once had for you is still present, but in the Friend-Zone is where we shall remain.

DON'T FAULT ANOTHER BLACK WOMAN FOR NOT BEING IN HER PRIME BECAUSE SHE'S IN AN UNFIT ENVIRONMENT. CHANGE HER ENVIRONMENT AND WATCH HER FLOURISH.

As long as she's in an unfit, limited environment, her mind will only go as far as that environment will allow her. Change her environment to a more efficient one, watch her mind becomes enriched and watch her produce phenomenal results.

What drives me crazy
is when black women who made it out of poor conditions,
criticize both younger and older women who are in their old shoes.

So you forgot where you came from?

The Black Woman Is God

The first human fossil found is of a black woman. It is the Black Woman who created life. I believe before the creation of man, a black woman (the Black Madonna) produced her child through a process called parthenogenesis, a form of reproduction in which an egg can develop into an embryo without being fertilized by a sperm (i.e. the Black Madonna and Child. Not the Virgin Mary). When the process died, man was created to assist in reproduction.

Other ethnic groups came after...

Men do not birth children; therefore, women do not come from men. X comes before Y and we know that women carry the X chromosome. There's no evidence of women coming from men. We know that men come from women (black women), we have breasts that don't produce milk and a reproductive organ (penis) similar to a woman's clitoris.

Before many of us acknowledged any religion, by nature as an infant/child, the only God we recognized was our mother. Not our father, not our sisters/brothers, but our mother. We craved her nursing, nurturing, direction and protection.

A black family is at its strongest and at its best when all the pieces are present; Queen, King and their offspring. The true Holy Trinity. The most powerful piece in a game of chess is the Queen. The most powerful person in the black family is the Queen. If they destroy the mind of the "black man" or destroy him physically, you remove the protection from the Queen who holds the true power, who is then destroyed by our oppressors through social engineering and propaganda.

I believe many men do not recognize the black woman as God or a Goddess, because the one they were supposed to have wasn't present, or if she was, she wasn't protected properly. Chess pieces being out of place. Many men shut black women out because of how their mother treated them.

I'm not saying black men aren't powerful, but we aren't as powerful as our black women. A black man who builds, leads, educates, protects, provides and serves his family as well as his community, puts his black woman first. At least I do, as well as those I know who actually put foot to pavement. You show me a strong successful brother; I will show you a more powerful black sister.

Most men produce offspring and run to the streets or into jail, while that powerful woman manages to take care of herself and her household. Any man who skips out on his child, who abuses women is a coward.

The black woman has the supernatural ability to bear pain. Despite what she has endured, what brothers do to them that is unpleasant, the burdens that society and the government has placed on her, she still rises. A weak brother on the other hand can't pull himself up from falling two inches in the mud without help from a black woman. Many don't have their own home and are living off a black woman. Many who get arrested, their first call goes to their child's mother whom they have failed or their own mother who they didn't listen to.

I have knowledge of self and knowledge of a woman. It is my duty to give credit where it is due and that is to my black women who've made the world what it is today, and who go out of their way to help make their household, community and world a better place.

I will continue to be honest and speak up for my sisters, which many men have failed to do. They were here first and they are the creators of life and founders of civilization. The Black Woman Is God.

The Black Woman Have Earned My Glory, Protection, Love and Support.

When I found her,
I wasn't looking for a completed puzzle.

But an incomplete one with a million pieces.

**One that I can
construct myself.**

One that I can call my own.

It is her right and her right only
to claim me as hers.

For **I only belong**
to her and no one else.

Your perception of Her
won't make me change
the way I value Her.

As she is for me and Not
You.

ONE OF THE MOST UNATTRACTIVE THINGS A WOMAN CAN DO IS TALK DOWN ON ANOTHER MAN'S WOMAN BECAUSE HE CHOSE HER INSTEAD.

What he sees in her is not what you see.
For him, it could be more than her appearance.

You can call her ugly or even talk about her hair and clothes, but she may have something within her that is way more valuable than anything that lies on the surface of hers and your skin, that is appealing to him.

On another note, **just because he didn't select you doesn't mean you aren't good enough; you are perfect for someone else.**

Just remember you don't have to belittle and degrade someone for securing your desire, because you won't be rewarded. Instead express gratitude for them both.

LADIES YOU HAVE NO RESPECT FOR YOURSELF, OUR CULTURE, YOUR DAUGHTER OR ANY OTHER BLACK WOMAN, BY REFERRING TO EACH OTHER AS BITCHES.

There are many positive adjectives that you
can use to refer to each other as, but instead
you rather continue to cater to our oppressors
plans of degrading and destroying our culture.

Nothing good is going to surface for you if you continue
to degrade your own.

Uplift and inspire each other. Love each other.
Replace Bitch with Beautiful.

ALL MY SISTERS
ARE BEAUTIFUL

Sisters, you all are Beautiful,
both inside and out.

Don't allow anyone to tell you any
different. I love each and
every one of you.

**Beauty is not just what you see,
it's what you feel. I feel the greatness
within you when I'm in your presence.**

Use your natural worth and gifts to
change the world in which we live.

Sisters, you are the most important
beings on this planet and it's important
that everyone you associate with,
acknowledge your presence as the life
of the Earth and the Queen of our destiny.

Without you, there is no life.

LOVE LOST and FOUND

If you don't need me,
then why are you even here?

My love and investment in you is much more than a liability!

Tell me, do I mean anything to you?
Tell me, do I?

Have you really received the love I have given you?

Do you even know what love is? What love looks and feels like?

You know what? Forget I even asked.

You should just pack your bags and go.

Leave the keys!

I'll keep the memories and lose you.

I no longer need you.

I need a woman who needs a man that needs her!

**My love for you is now lost, but it shall be found within her
who I need and she who needs me.**

Oh, You Independent Independent!

Never Depend On A Man!

But why ask a man for a job?

Never Depend On A Man!

But why ask him to look at or fix your car?

Never Depend On A Man!

But why purchase his products/services?

Never Depend On A Man!

Buy why lease his property?

Never Depend On A Man!

But why ask to borrow his money?

Some of the things you need and desire in life,
you have to depend on someone to obtain them.

**So, be mindful of trying to be too independent
because you need others in order to survive.**

Hey Single Mothers,

You may not need a man, but your children do.

Why must your children be without full mental, emotional and spiritual support from their father, guardian, or male role model because you want to be independent?

It takes both a man and a woman to teach children certain things, preparing them for life. Men can teach your daughter things that you aren't able to teach. Just like you are able to teach your son things his father can't.

Find your children male leaders. You don't have to invite their male role model into your home or bedroom.

Don't Allow Your Daughter
to Be in the Presence of A Man
Who Doesn't Treat
Her Mother Right,
Because She Will Only Grow Up Allowing
Herself to Be Mistreated by A Man
Just Like Her Mother.

ALL OF US AREN'T DOGS.
THE ONES YOU'VE DATED ARE.

WHEN YOU BELIEVE A LITTLE
GREATER, YOU ATTRACT GREATER.

So, since you already have your mind set
on all men aren't good, you
will only attract those who really aren't.

#LawofAttraction

MESSAGE TO MY SISTERS

Sisters, uplift our black brothers.

Speak life into them and encourage them to achieve something greater than their eyes can see?

LET'S GET RID OF THE DESTRUCTIVE CRITICISM.
NO MORE DEGRADING OF OUR BLACK MEN.

There is no worse feeling than our woman not supporting our work and criticizing us destructively.

Our biggest concern already, is trying to survive in a world setup for us to fail, and to have our woman not support us or our work is just as heavy.

We work hard at what we value, and to have the closest person to us, criticize it without support can make us react in ways we didn't intend to react. The tongue of a woman is her weapon against man and she doesn't know how badly it affects him until the end result. When he attempts to address the situation, his feelings or concerns, and she opens her mouth with her razor tongue, it cuts deep hitting a major artery.

Johann Wolfgang Von Goethe says, **"When we treat a man as he is, we make him worse than he is; when we treat him as if he already were what he potentially could be, we make him what he should be."**

Speak his purpose into existence. Speak life into Him. Use Positive Affirmations and Support Him to the Best of Your Ability.

Set Yourself Free... Set Him Free and FLY!

Cater to the Nature of Man!

"Cater to Man?" - I'm not referring to just the brushing of our hair, cleaning behind us, rubbing our backs, etc. That is superficial.

Catering to the nature of man is catering to his core principles in which lies beneath the surface.

How are you tapping into his spirit?
Do you possess mental and physical attractiveness?
Are you his true friend and confidant?
Or do your family and friends know all of his business?
Do you adhere to his sexual desires and appetite?
Or is he brushed away negatively and fed the same stuff?
Do you consider his thoughts, emotions, pain, values, dreams, etc.?
Or is it all about you?

Catering to the nature of men is essential for that man to provide you the life you require.

Ladies, when a guy approaches you wrongly, instead of degrading, belittling, and bashing him on social media or to anyone else, correct him so that his next approach is successful, whether is during a conversation or he is asking you or another woman out. If you are already involved with someone, kindly let him know and show him how to properly address a woman so that he can properly ask her out.

"Break the cycle of degrading our brothers who haven't been properly taught how to address and communicate with a woman."

If a male, whether someone you know or a stranger, young or older fail to open the door for you, demand that he opens the door for you. He may have never been taught the importance of being a gentleman. Therefore, he will know that he has to open the door the nest time. **Don't be okay with allowing the door to slam on you or on your heels.**

"Teach our young and older men how a woman is supposed to be treated so that they will treat the next woman with respect. Don't adopt the attitude of he should already know because it's a learned behavior, it's not something we were born with and we know many of our men were raised by Single Mothers."

As long as you seek for and confirm him
as your nigga, you will always be treated
less than a woman deserves to be treated.

**Seek a nigga, attract a nigga, be with a nigga
and you will be treated exactly how that nigga
treated his previous encounters.**

ELEVATE YOUR PREFERENCES.

A good woman is not a woman
who refers to her man as her nigga.

Nor would she allow anyone else to label
him as such. **Nor would she use the term to
identify another man or her son.**

ALLOWING HIM TO LABEL YOU AS HIS GIRLFRIEND IS A LOW VIBRATION.

ELEVATE YOUR TITLE.

You are a **Lady**, You are a **Woman**,
You are a **Princess**, You are a **Duchess**,
You are a **Queen**.

YOU ARE NOT YOUR DAUGHTER,
YOU ARE NOT A GIRL.

Ladies,
if he is not providing the security you need,
why are you risking your life staying with him?

Ladies,
if your man doesn't lie down with you and hold you after y'all finish business, there's a poor connection in his spirit and

It's Time to Give Him a Reality Check.

If his spirit is well and yours is too, lying with you right after allows you to pour the necessary energy into him to go on and conquer his destiny, and to tackle the obstacles that may stand in the way.

Him being with you right after (if he is right) will allow him to pour the required energy into you so that you can recharge your nurturing control center, which allows you to be merciful; forgiving, compassionate, loving and caring. Not to just him, but to yourself and others.

Most men are manipulators at heart.

They prey upon weak and broken women with no intentions of helping them heal or no intentions of staying with them for long periods of time. No Sustainability. **A manipulative male knows when a woman is broken and will decide to feed her his Tylenol that will temporarily numb the pain that she have been experiencing, while tricking her mind to give up the best of her.** He knows that if he pretends to give even a slight more dosage of care, compassion, understanding and respect than her ex, she will eventually open her heavens gates and welcome him inside. He knows that she will grow to be attached to him.

After effortlessly gaining access inside her body without any requirement on her part for him to put forth any effort, the dosage of his Tylenol becomes less and less, causing her numbness to wear off; resulting in her experiencing the pain that she felt once before; from her new pharmacist this time.

Manipulative men have ill intentions from the start and have no true desire to truly help women who have been broken heal or evolve. He knows that such women would soon be attached to him after being prescribed his acetaminophen and he wouldn't be attached to them, which would make it easier for him to detach from them. He knew he would leave her for someone else to fix while moving on to his next victim after achieving his mission of luring her into his trap to quickly gain her trust, her body and everything else, and robbing her of the little good she had left.

Sister, you are #Valuable.

You are worth more than any Jewel and if you've
given yourself to someone who haven't earned you,
it's okay. It's time to remind you of your worth.

**You are God; you are the Earth, the Sun, the Moon,
the Stars and the Sea. No man deserves all of that who
haven't earned it.**

A man whom you find attractive shouldn't enter your
most sacred, but precious gift because of his attractiveness.

But because he has knowledge of self, his history, his culture,
has proven to be responsible and capable of leading you,
building you, educating you, protecting you, providing for you
and serving you.

By the time he gets to you, he should have completed your training
academy.

You did the right thing by **letting him go** and moving forward with Someone who **represents you well.**

Ladies,

just because the guy that you want doesn't like you back,
doesn't mean that you aren't beautiful. **You are.**

Don't kill yourself.

Millions of sperms compete amongst each other
to get to the Ovum.

Out of millions, it's only one that is able to fertilize
the egg to create life.

The ovum don't swim to the sperm, so a female
shouldn't be driving a male to prom.

A female shouldn't be taking 100% care of a man and **she
damn sure shouldn't be throwing herself at millions of guys.**

The right one will swim up if you are patient, prepared and ready.

Don't attempt to race your ovum toward the sperm because that's
not your place. Especially if they haven't swum towards you anyway.

Ladies, don't allow a materialistic thing which hold no true value cause you to miss out on someone worthy.

Also, **don't allow a shiny thing to blind you, preventing you from seeing one's true colors,** because there are men out here who will put on a mask and play on your vulnerability with gifts or not, leading you into their torture chamber.

Ladies, when you become emotionally disconnected,
you have to develop self-discipline and give yourself time to heal. At this
state of distress, you are emotionally needy and your emotions may have
taken the place of your intelligence. When your emotions are in control,
you may be subjected to do anything to numb the pain.

When you are at your lowest, there will be men who will try to play on
your emotions in order to sleep with you, creating more damage than has
already been done. They will approach you with sweet talks; ask to take
you out for dinner and drinks, and to be invited to your place. **When they
do, decline. Also, your girlfriends may try to get you to date a guy
who they believe is a good fit for you. Decline. You should focus on
trying to heal.** You aren't ready to be dating. You want to make yourself
available (not sexually) to those who have interest in restoring you to your
original state of being. Not blinding you with food and alcohol thinking
it's a First Aid Kit that will heal the damage that has been done.

When you are at your weakest, develop the strength to stand on your
feet. Develop the strength to discipline yourself to close the door to your
bedroom, your body and liquor agencies. Getting your womb massaged
won't heal you from the pain. Instead, it may hurt you even more,
especially if you let that person in and he didn't plan on staying. Develop
the strength to seek love and empathy from your true friends and loved
ones so that you can be restored back to the true you and may enjoy your
purposeful life.

When he invests in your goals and dreams,
make your problems his and helps you overcome them,
He's the one.

Ladies,

Be mindful of Boys who will try to Discredit Your Man So They Can Get You.

Opening your mind to the negative influences of others will prevent you from creating a deeper connection with the one you are with.

Good men won't try to take you from someone you are currently involved with (who is treating you well), just so they can have you.

That's a negative tendency.

Don't be moved by money, sweet talks and expensive items. **It's a Trap.**

Dear Ladies,

A perfect guy isn't going to fall out of the sky and into your arms, if you aren't preparing yourself for him. Carrying yourself unpleasantly will only attract those men who are unpleasant, but who appears to be worthy in the beginning. "MASK-ON"

Many of you are focused on big things that don't really matter and not seeing the little things that matter the most. Open your eyes!

Carry yourself how a woman should at all times, learn how to prepare yourself for the perfect man and learn how to weed out men who aren't beneficial to your existence.

Chapter 6: You've Been Dating Wrong, So Date Right "Cultivating Minds To Own Thyself"

Why Do Black Men Begin To Lack Intimacy and Sex While In A Relationship With A Black Woman?

America is a battlefield for Blacks, especially for black men. The moment his mother (especially if she was young) found out she was pregnant; he was already programmed for failure. Young mothers are often found delivering low-birth weight babies, which results in him growing up with learning deficiencies. Young boys with learning deficiencies are often found in single mother homes, in poverty dominated neighborhoods. Many single mother homes don't have a foundation of academic and economic education, intimacy, compassion, love and respect. As a result, young boys fall behind in school, become distant from love, affection from women, and eventually end up on the streets, fostering a life of drugs, alcohol and criminal activity, in which many end up in the jail and prison system.

There are little to no resources or programs in these neighborhoods that are working toward reversing the current conditions of blacks. When black boys and men are denied that opportunity to learn, earn a living, raise a family and live rewarding lives like the top people in America, nobody cares, let alone help. Not even black women. America has designed this way of life for us. Many of us have become immune to a life of hopelessness, betrayal, and defeat to that point we can no longer recognize ourselves in the mirror. We can't recognize people who are here to help.

Those of us who have managed to avoid a life of incarceration, who have managed to get an education and to secure a position with a company, are in the most danger. One slip up at a job can get us fired. One slip up of yelling at our lady can get us thrown in jail. Without a job, we have no money or transportation, which makes it harder to find another place of employment. Being jobless, we still need to eat, need a place to stay and have to manage other responsibilities. With domestic violence on our record, although it was verbal, it costs us everything. Why? Verbal domestic violence isn't stated on your record; it just shows Domestic Violence. Society would already assume you beat up your wife. **No job, No money, No home, No driver's license, a Criminal Record, and No Woman, Back to The Ghetto We Go, with anyone who will allow us to sleep on the floor. We then go into survival mode, developing animal like instincts, being the predator and being preyed upon until we are buried in the ground or escorted to the impound.**

This is why many of us black men lack sex and intimacy in our relationships. We can't escape the harsh realities of life. There's no freedom. Most of our women don't understand that. Oftentimes, when we do attract a woman who we think is worthy of assisting us in being free from this hellhole, she winds up not better than our oppressors. She gives us right back to the slave owner whose plantation we have escaped from. She's unaware of the trapped corners everywhere we go and if she is, she does nothing to help break the trap. Most women are blinded by their own future, fame, glamor, problems, emotions, and responsibilities to the point that they fail to ignore the personal problems their black men are experiencing.

Black men aren't going to be affectionate or be involved sexually with our woman if they have something bothering them on the lines of finances, racism and the fear of failure, and their women are doing nothing to help. Society has programmed many of us to keep what's bothering us inside and not share it to the possibility of humiliation, especially from a black woman. This causes us to become distant from love and affection.

When a black man is working on himself, trying to reach certain milestones or is in a lost or very emotional place, intimacy and sex is limited, your job as a woman is to study his behavior and figure how he can gain your trust so that he can share with you what's wrong. Once he does, it's imperative that you share it with nobody because he will never trust you again. Also, once he reveals himself, you should try to help cater to his needs. Help him heal!

"A woman who doesn't make his problems hers, is a woman who will soon be without him." This is the reality of most of our people. This is why men are who they are and why women are who they are. No one wants to make the other person's problems theirs or help repair them.

I've learned on my personal journey that, sometimes we have to step outside of ourselves and step into the other person and shine the operating room light on them. When we are so caught up in ourselves, we lose sight of the other person; their needs, wants and desires. We take a good person and make them bad because we have failed to respond to their needs appropriately.

A child is unable to explain how he feels, but in most cases as a parent, you know what he needs when he is whiny or what he wants when he is giggly. We seem to have lost that connection with adult on adult interactions. Verbal communication alone can be a diversion from the real problem. A patient who suffers from a mental illness can tell you that she's okay but in reality, you know she's not. We have to go beneath the surface of words and correct the problem at hand which involves observation, behavior analysis, and treatment.

"You can't make a person happy. They have to already be happy inside." That applies when you first meet them! But, what happens when that spark leaves? Are we supposed to restore that on our own if the rest of the world already ignores our problems like they do to the rest of us? Our woman is supposed to ignore it as well?

Sisters, we are a unit and we need each other to overcome obstacles. I can almost guarantee that, if our problems become yours and yours become ours within the relationship and we work toward fixing them, you will have your abundance of intimacy, love, joy, loyalty and sex. But for now, if your black man is off track, help him restore his balance if he is willing.

On my way in her DM to remind her of her worth,
**in efforts of her taking the initiative to clear her
conscious and vision** so she can be restored to her
original state of being.
Happy and at Peace.

PROMISES

When we met, you told me that you've been hurt and abandoned by those who were supposed to love and be there for you.

You asked me to make a promise to love you unconditionally and to promise you that I will never hurt nor leave you.

I made a promise to never harm you with my words or actions and that I will never
leave you, but will protect you.

I promised you that I will love you with every inch of me. I've done that and stayed true to my promise.

Out of nowhere, you asked me to leave.
I put up a fight to stay and yet you pushed me away.

He wasn't what you expected and now you have returned to the same doormat you stood on when you wiped your feet clean of the best I've given you.

Where were your promises?

How could you be so blinded of the masterpiece that stood before you, right before you turned away, showing me the back of your mini dress, the one I had purchased for your commencement dinner and before the heel of your shoe scraped off the curb as you entered his car?

I prepared myself for me and then I prepared myself for you. **Then you prepared yourself for him who just wanted a spoon full of what I thought was only prepared for me forever.**

And now, you want me to eat it like you have never had it eaten before and make your body tremble from a massive orgasm only I've been able to give you.

You want me to give you what I once had given you and you know what?

I promise you!

I promise you that... that will never happen again.

I will not give you the luxury of hurting and abandoning me again like the ones you cried to me about as I comforted you when you and I first met.

I promise you that,
you aren't worthy
of me Again!

03

HIM

Do you know what a cactus and a strong black woman have in common?

They both have a hard shell protecting their most prized possessions.

But if you cut them right and treat them right, they will cum for you in ways you didn't know they could cum.

Their ingredients can rehydrate you and save your life.

The mother of your children
deserves happiness and joy;

**don't kill me for uncovering her
smile that you had hidden.**

I took her mind off the pain
that you inflicted.

**Now she's rejoicing in my
world of pleasure.**

A Woman Is Not A Bitch!

If she doesn't appoint you, it doesn't mean that she's a bitch.

It just means that, **she made the right move to ensure she didn't allow one on her side.**

If you do your part, a Queen will ensure you get appointed as her king. be treated as a king and will allow you to remain her king.

No one truly knows what we experience because
our experiences are only for us to experience.

Society has moved away from being empathic and
compassionate towards the feelings of others, especially
Black Men.

When we express our emotions from all the pressure society
has placed upon us, they label us as being weak, being a "bitch."

In the real sense, **the weak man is the man who is afraid to show
emotion because of how he thinks society will react to him.**

He's controlled by what people think, say and do, which draws
him from expressing himself freely.

As men, we have the right to express ourselves, our pain freely
and it's unrighteous for society to bash us for how we express our pain.

TAKE ACCOUNTABILITY

**You can no longer blame businesses
for not giving you a job, for reasons
of dealing drugs, robbing individuals and
burglarizing homes.**

Create your own business just as business owners
have done, or develop enough skills to secure employment
and provide for you and your family.

You cannot blame your last girlfriend or
wife for your reasons of not loving again.
You cannot blame your mother for not showing
you affection. Stand up and seek knowledge on
the subject of love and be all that you can be.

MESSAGE TO MY BROTHERS

Brothers, respect, love, support, protect
and care for our children and sisters.

Help provide protection in your
homes and communities.

Be leaders in your home and in the community.

NO MORE BEING DISRESPECTFUL TO OUR WOMEN.
NO MORE ABANDONING OF OUR CHILDREN.
NO MORE BEING SELFISH.

Fellas,

The role we play in our child's/children's life from birth to adolescent years will determine which path they take in life.

It's important that we continue to be leaders in our home and in our community.

Don't just be dads to your biological children, but to the children of others, especially those in your community. They need you; your direction, your energy and your control.

It's imperative that we express the same amount of love and affection to our children as we express discipline. There has to be a balance. Our children are missing your love.

It's not just mom job to kiss and hug, it's your job as well. Love your child and the children of others, so they can grow to love others.

Correct and praise for small things, as well as for big things. Celebrate their small accomplishments.

Discipline them, correct them and love them afterwards. This method develops their respect for you and helps them enhance their direction in life.

SINGLE FATHERS,

You May Not Need A Woman, But Your Children Do!

Why must your children be without full mental, emotional
and spiritual support from their mother, guardian or
female role model because you want to be independent?

It takes both a man and a woman to teach children certain things,
preparing them for life. Women can teach your son things that you
aren't able to teach. Just like you can teach your daughter things her
mother can't.

Find your children female leaders. You don't have to invite their female
role model into your home or your bedroom.

At times, when you know a woman is vulnerable,

Don't Play On Her Weakness.

Instead, show empathy, love and guide her.

No other woman can carry our tradition and legacy like our own women. No other woman can care for and protect us like our own women. No other woman will stand up and fight the enemy like our women. There are no other women fighting to restore us back to our original state of being like our own women.

Many of our men see many of the problems many of our women endure and say to themselves, "she has too many problems on her hands," "I'm not dealing with her mess," or "she has an attitude problem," and run away taking the easy way out by dating and marrying someone outside of our culture. Leaving our women to endure more. These men are weak; yeah I said it, "Weak."

They are afraid and are too lazy to help rebuild our queens to their original state of being because it requires too much work on their part. Instead, they want the easy way out, everything handed to them. So, they go on and seek someone outside of our culture who doesn't have it so hard, who would obey every command of theirs because black women won't. They are afraid of the challenges that come with the black woman, which makes them weak. Challenges that are actually good for them, because **if they were to help black women through their challenges, black women would come back at them with a love they have never felt before in their life. A love no other woman from another race could provide.**

If they weren't afraid and accepted the challenge, it will help them get the proper love and direction they require.

WOMEN WITH CHILDREN
HAVE BENEFITS

Fellas,

Maybe a woman with a child or children
will help you develop good character traits
and will inspire you to become who you are
destined to become.

I told myself, I would never date a woman with
children. After analyzing what I had said, it was
a selfish thought.

Kids aren't asked to come into this world and it is
not their fault that their father either was killed,
went to jail or just refused to take care of them.

They need good men in their lives that can teach
them the importance of love, integrity, respect and
many other life skills. Being a role model to the children
of others have helped me become a better man.

I'm a father to every child I encounter. It takes a
community to raise a child and I'm that cool guy
up the block.

So, don't limit yourself to just a woman without kids.

As long as you continue to allow her to refer to you as a nigga,
she will never fully respect you, your son, her son or and other men.

Allowing you to be labeled as a nigga is a low vibration.

CORRECT HER OR DROP HER!

ELEVATE YOUR TITLE!

ALLOWING HER TO LABEL YOU AS HER BOYFRIEND IS A LOW VIBRATION.

ELEVATE YOUR TITLE.

The term "Boy" is used to label grown men,
to keep them in a childlike mentality.

**Slave Owners referred to Grown, Strong,
Intelligent Black Men as Boys to keep black
men believing that they are inferior to white men.**

Boy is what we refer to our sons as.
We aren't boys, we are men.

"DEMAND YOUR RESPECT"

If you are willing to put all of her pieces
back together, She Can Become Whole Again.

If She is Willing To Be Helped.

Him

You aren't going to secure her with
consistent kissy faces or emoji heart
faced texts.

But you can secure her **if you can prove
to her that you can add value to her** current state
of being and stay consistent after you provide
the first layer of value.

Her body belongs to her.
Not you.

It's up to her if she desire
to share it with you.

If you are even **worthy of it.**

When she fuels your passion and desire
to become better, **she is the one.**

If you lead right, she will follow.

Allow her to shadow your steps,
then allow her to lead too.

She will lead you to your destiny.

This is her world; **she knows the way.**

The world doesn't have to know how much she means to you **as long as she knows how much she means to you.**

You aren't with her for the world's approval.

She desired to give me what she have
that is yours.

But, she remembered her vows and
went Home.

She Loves You.

DEAR MAN,

Sometimes you'll just be too much a man.

Too wise, too handsome, too strong, too confident,
too visionary, and too outgoing.

Too much of a man that makes a woman feel like
she isn't worthy of you, **which will start making you
feel like you have to be less of a man in order for the
woman who lacks the ability to elevate to have you.**

One of the biggest mistakes you can make as a man,
is demoting your worth and potential for a woman
who isn't equipped to wear the crown that matches
your position as King.

You do not need to devalue yourself to be in the presence
of a woman. You need a woman who increases your current value.

DEAR FATHERS

It's not often that fathers, who are the true leaders of society, whose existence is necessary for the advancement and livelihood of our species, have a moment where the light is shined upon them. Light honoring our existence and role as a builder, leader, educator, protector and provider to our children.

Most of the light is shined upon the mothers, which leaves us in the shadow as they reap all the honors. But for my fellow fathers, your efforts of being a better man, and an even better father doesn't go unnoticed. Some of our greatest masterpieces were created in the dark.

Today, the light is shining upon you and I'm taking this opportunity to thank you for your continuous love, honor, effort, respect, commitment, time, and generosity that you share not just with your biological child (ren), but with your grandchildren and the children of others.

Also, I would like to thank you for your help in making this world a better place, by raising your child (ren) to be well-mannered, well-behaved, intelligent and responsible.

Fellas, the light is never really turned off, folks just choose not to admire our greatness because they may be self-centered and envious of our greatness as men.

I Love You All, World's
Greatest Fathers.

I belong to me and no one else.
Whom I share me with is my decision by divine right.
No transfer of ownership have been made and no invoice
payment for property taxes have been received.

04

BEDROOM BOOM

"Securing an intimate relationship with someone worthy is a great milestone to reach, but that shouldn't be where your eyes shut. There's so much more to achieve during your time here; become more optimistic, keep your vision alive and attract more. Even after you secure your intimate relationship."

If You Aren't Able to Attract Them with Your Intelligence, Don't Lose Your Value by Offering Your Body for Free.

OLD SOUL LIVING

I think my biggest flaw is, "living too fast," growing older quick.
But, I refuse to think small and live for moments
that give me no opportunities to exist.

Like, I've always loved older people. In fact, they are my favorite people.
But, when they call me young man,
I kind of get upset because I see them as my equal.

I was more of a man than most men when I was 26,
wise beyond my time and I've coached men over 46.

But, she still insists I'm too young;
like my mother's friends and older cousins' ex-girlfriends when I was very
young. Now that I'm older, your chances are slim to none.

You should have just waited,
waited for me to blossom into this seed of greatness.
But for you, you were very impatient.
Anxious for your temporary forevers,
I still wish you well in all your future endeavors,
but we shall never be together.

So, just let me live in my old ways, no need for me to be stuck on one wave,
my grand-folks would say, "You have your whole life ahead of you".

LESSONS FROM GRANDMA

*"The best way to his heart his through his Grandmother.
If you haven't taken the time to schedule a sit down with me to gather
my recipe and the gps coordinates to his control center while I'm still alive
and well, your chances at success with my grandson may be shot."*

My grandma have taught me what love looks and feels like from a woman, and that if a woman cannot treat me as good as she treats me, then that woman isn't worthy of me. My grandma have never lifted a finger to harm me, only to hug and to hold me. My grandma have never fixed her lips to yell at me in anger or to slander my name, only to build me up and cheer me on from the sideline and in the stands.

My grandma once told me, "get to the point in life where people must come correct or don't come at all. You shall not accept nor tolerate the uncontrolled emotions and behaviors of women and others. Once you are at that point, you will be able to see and move toward a brighter path ahead." She continued by saying, "another woman's mother or father issues is not your problem. That is her problem. She shall take it amongst herself to heal her wounds and meet you where you stand as a mature, educated, successful and responsible adult, or don't come at all." If you allow her to come and stay, and she haven't met you where you stand, she will soon impose her problems onto you for you to fix, which will weigh down your crown which she cannot help you pick up. She will then start to hate you for your failed attempts and blame you for all the problems her parents, previous boyfriends and husbands have caused her.

*"If she cannot treat you nearly as good as I treat you or
as good as you treat yourself, then she isn't worthy of you.
Whenever, she fixes her mouth to speak unkindly to and
of you, it's time to Go!"*

Woman was created for man and man was created for woman, but an intimate relationship isn't essential for life. It's a choice you make and you can change your decision whenever you desire. If you have a healthy relationship, you may want to hold onto it, if you wish. If it's an unhealthy one, be on the next flight out.

Grandson, never allow anyone to put you in position where you can jeopardize what you have by doing something you do not wish to do. This is your life and you are in control of it.
So Own It!

You cannot be mad at a person for revealing their true colors
when you didn't require them to reveal them **when you first met them.**

You and I knew they **weren't the one when we** met them. We pretended to be blindfolded (Bird Box) to their Red Flags with the idea that **they would change for us.**

We Chose to Stay.

We Chose to Walk on the Line of Fire.

We harmed ourselves when we **Removed the Blindfold** after the **Honeymoon Phase.**

Our Blindfold Should Have Been Removed from the Beginning.

Shattered!

TRAPPED IN LUST

You're advertising to the world that you two are going through some things;
instead of patching things up, you run and tell the next candidate
everything that's going wrong, but only your side of the story.

Saddened by your story, you guys meet over a glass of wine.
You're blinded by their blurred lines.

They're telling you all these wonderful things,
just so they can get some of that thang,
so you can snuggle that thang in your warm moist place.

I'm talking about that thing between your thighs that is placed between
those thighs that make you sigh, "my, my, my", that make you cry in a
pool of pleasure.

**That thirst for that quick fix, that thirst for that drip drip.
That drunk in love without a glove, had you feeling like you were in love.
Now. those poison fluids got you sick quick.**

That STD got you living in fear.
Now you're trapped up alone with an unhappy career.

You are spending life in and out of beds, thinking the answer is opening legs,
massaging heads, I mean massaging your mind.
Now you're paying out of pocket, "thank you for your time, I'll see you
next week."

Now she's saying to herself, "if I have his baby he'll stay,
cook and clean for him, he'll stay."
But he didn't stay, so she got on her knees to pray,
that everything will be okay. And still. things aren't okay.

He's saying, "well, if I buy her earrings, if I buy her everything, tell her
nice things, she'll fall in love with me,
or maybe, just maybe she will love me forever."
But she won't.

Settling just for that exterior attraction
WILL GET YOU HURT QUICK

Dig Deeper.

Don't Date Liabilities,
date Assets.

Invest In You.

THIRSTY

Being thirsty for someone is an instant gratification
that (more often than not), results in you quenching
individuals that may not be good for you, which still
leave you with a feeling of thirst.

Like a drink, when you have it in your possession and you
are thirsty, you consume the contents immediately without the
thought of sustainability or the affect it may have on your health.
You get a refill because you aren't satisfied and then you consume
more until your belly is full.

**Consuming a person's contents rapidly, then discarding
them and thirsting for another person with the hopes of that
person satisfying your thirst is harmful.** Your thirst will not be
quenched, because you have consumed all of their contents without
thinking about sustaining them, without checking their nutritional label
and without giving yourself time to recuperate.

Instead of being thirsty for someone, learn to be savoring with
the purpose of sustaining, so you can hold on to them for a lifetime.

THE INTERVIEW

Me: Thank you for expressing your interest in me. Your interview went well. However, I will keep your application on a file and I will get back to you within a couple of weeks with my decision. I have a few more candidates to interview before I make my final decision.

I'll be in touch, Okay?

Candidate: Ok.

TWO WEEKS LATER

"Phone Ring"

Candidate: Hi, I'm calling to check on the status of my application.

Me: What's your name?

Hi yes, I was scheduled to call you this evening. But now that I have you here,
due to your background check, the falsification on your application and your most recent case of negativity and degradation of black men, I have chosen a more qualified candidate for the position.

However, you may apply again within 60 days, this person may not last.

Don't put your child (ren) in danger for Lust. Lust isn't more important than the safety of your children.

Check your persons of interest background history; criminal clearance and child abuse record. You don't want to risk dating people for six months or more and find out they have an extensive criminal background, along with child related charges.

Don't risk leaving your child alone with or sitting on the lap of sexual predators or those who harm children. Your persons of interest should be a great leader and role model for you as well as your children.

Fellas, your lady should be, nurturing the nation and supporting you to the best of her ability.

Ladies, your guy should be a builder, a leader, an educator, a protector, provider, and server to his family as well as his community.

IF YOU ONLY SEE THE PERSON YOU ARE INVOLVED WITH FOR THE MOMENT AND NOT THE LONG RUN, LET THEM GO.

They deserve someone who's more visionary and who breathes longevity.

"I'M NOT YOUR INSTANT WINNING SCRATCH OFF"

Within your approach, if you believe all of me will be deposited into you within a short period of time, think again because it's not going to happen.

This doesn't mean that I'm not interested in you; it means that great things are secured with time, effort, dedication and persistence. Like a business, we can't be built without a foundation and a foundation can't be built overnight. Especially not under extreme weather conditions.

This also doesn't mean that I expect to get your complete investment within the first 48 hours. **Because I have to invest time and effort into you as well**; not only to prove myself worthy, but to understand each of your layers that makes you, and to secure the right pieces in your perfect 25,000 piece puzzle.

So, instant gratification and success is not my plan; I'm not looking to win your jackpot with luck and you shouldn't look to secure mine with one lucky spin, but with hard work and efforts of sustaining our existence, while maximizing our potential and successes as a unit. **Longevity**

The first step in dating isn't securing what you desire;
**it's forming a connection with a person or persons
of interest with efforts of building a solid foundation
of friendship.**

You can't build a facility without forming its foundation first.

It's nice to look at its picture, floor plan and blueprints,
but if the dirt hasn't been removed from the potential
building ground, it will always remain and idea.

After the foundation is set, then it would be safe to build the
third layer of the building; in this case, the relationship.

Date, become friends and then form the relationship.

SOMEONE MAY BE RIGHT FOR YOU BUT YOU MAY NOT BE RIGHT FOR THEM

Just because you express your interest in someone
who carry themselves as how a man or
woman should, **doesn't mean they are obligated to
make themselves available for you.**

They may be right for you, but you may not be right
for them. Please understand that.

Also, understand that one may not be able to accept you
because you haven't healed from your previous injuries
and is still trying to jump tree to tree. And with each leap,
you come crashing down.

Time heals wounds and if you don't invest time in healing
before jumping again, you won't ever get far.

Playing on a broken ankle before it fully
recover will only make it worse.

Let your wounds heal before trying to run a new marathon.
If not, you will only experience sprints in your relationships.

You want me; All OF ME.

You want me mentally, physically, emotionally, spiritually and sexually.

You want me because I've grown into a mature, educated, successful and responsible adult.

You want me because I invest time in conversing with you, educating you; elevating your spirit and helping you bring out the best parts of you.

You want me because I possess certain traits and abilities you desire that was absent in your father, children's father and/or ex-partners.

You want me because I possess the love they have failed to give you.

You want me; ALL OF ME!

You want me to gently insert my member into your vagina, softly massaging it while passionately kissing your lips.

You want to cream me like Alfredo then, layup, eat dinner and watch movies with me daily.

You want me, but you haven't proposed anything else?

What about me? What about real relationship goals?

You have asked to fill the shoes that you aren't certain you would be able to fill based on the emotional experiences you are experiencing. What you are feeling emotionally is real; happiness, joy, good vibes, the urge to become better and no one can take that feeling from you. As a result of my genuineness and positive energy, I understand the emotions I have assisted you in developing, which is supposed to allow you to experience the feelings the way you are experiencing them. I have prepared myself to be this way.

Am I supposed to give myself away that easily? Just drop everything and run to you because you are lusting for me? What about my son, my family, close friends and business ventures? Did you factor in all of that or did you just think about securing me for yourself for a brief moment? That's right, a brief moment.

Your gloomy eyes are only open wide enough to see the honeymoon phase. Have you done your homework on me? Am I really who I put myself out to be? Did you fact check?

Falling in love with potential is dangerous and you have become blinded by potential, the potential of us being together with no real effort invested to ensure we are even a good fit.

What you are experiencing, the butterflies are temporary. It won't last forever.

If I gave you me at your request to fulfill your temporary fantasy, it wouldn't be long before you grow to become upset with me and maybe angry because nothing lasts forever, right? Have you prepared yourself for the rainy days?

When those temporary feelings of happiness fade away, then what? Will you still want me then?

Do you have what it takes to help restore us back to a happy place, or will you just run away and slander my name because things didn't go your way? Have you thought about sustainability? What about compromising? **What about competency in terms of settling our problems in-house rather than sharing them with your friends, family and the rest of the world?**

Despite wanting me mentally, physically, emotionally, spiritually and sexually, how can you invest in each of the following areas that are of importance to me **while still taking care of your own responsibilities, things and people that are of importance to you?**

1.   Me
2.   My Children
3.   Business Ventures
4.   My Family
5.   My Friends
6.   The Community

What is your plan for us merging our families, and distributing love, time, affection, attention and resources to everyone involved? **What is your plan for creating a better life for all of us? Have you thought about that?**

You must know that **my appetite goes well beyond a physical, mental, emotional, spiritual, and sexual attraction.** Good looks, a healthy mind and spirit, and sex could and will never be enough.

Relationship shouldn't be free flowing and many fail because they are. They should have a structure like a business; values, morals, principles and goals. Love is Law (universal) and family is business. If you don't have the blueprints, building permits and contracts, it won't be built properly; business will not flourish.

Take some time to think this through and stop allowing yourself to experience 40-yard dashes in your relationships. Create a blueprint for your potential relationship and a contract. Negotiate terms, date long-term, love freely, work together and grow.

One of the best things two people can have
is an understanding.

Once an understanding is present, the foundation
can begin to form.

Lovers can't be enemies. Oil and water don't mix.

Think about how long it took for you to get to know you;
now factor in how long it's going to take for you to get to know
someone else.

STOP TRYING TO GET 100% OF SOMEONE IN 15 DAYS.

PREPARE YOURSELF FOR THE ONE YOU HAVE BEEN WAITING FOR

There are many Women who want
a loving and responsible Man, **but
she isn't that loving and responsible
Woman for that Man.**

There are many Men who want
a loving and responsible Woman,
**but he isn't that loving and responsible
Man for that Woman.**

The creator will not place a good
partner before you, if you aren't
prepared to receive that individual.
He will not allow you to hurt that
individual that you are waiting for.

You must prepare yourself physically,
mentally, socially, emotionally and
spiritually for that individual.

Just like you have to work hard for your personal
success, you have to work hard for that individual.

The Way You Love May not be the way the Next Person Loves!

We must share with others how we wish to be loved, not how other people are loved on social media and on TV, but how we truly desire to be loved, because someone can be expressing their love for you in ways that you can't recognize because they have a different love language.

"A woman knows how she want to be loved and treated, and it's important that she teaches the man in her life how she want to be loved, instead of waiting on him to do something he's never going to do. **He may have loved another woman one way, but the love he gave that woman may not be the love that you require.** Every woman isn't loved the same. In return, that man should rise to the occasion. Vice Versa."

If you do not know how you wish to be loved, then it's important that you spend some time alone! You have to be in-tune with yourself first before trying to be in-tune with someone else.

While on your self-discovery of love, you must understand your deepest thoughts, desires, and emotions, your character traits, your values, what makes you happy and why you think and do the things you think and do (Quassim Cassam).

Once you have figured you out, then you will know how you desire to be loved and will be able to communicate that with others. It will be safe for you to learn someone else and their love language.

If you do not know who you are, you will find it extremely difficult fusing your soul with another. You may find yourself blaming everyone else but you for the downfall of your relationships.

While on your personal discovery, purchase a journal and pen and begin documenting you. Share it with your person of interest. It can possibly assist them in learning how to love you effectively.

BAGGAGE CLAIM

Many people desire to have a good partner.
Many of those same people don't know how
to treat and/or keep that good person.

Often times, they slam the door in the face
of those who are willing to love them fully;
damaging them because of past failed relationships.

Work on preparing you for that good
individual and learn how to keep them good
once you have them in your possession.

To my Good People, **the worst thing you can do
as a good person is**, claim someone else's dirty
baggage at baggage claim.

Attract your person of interest through
confidence and intelligence.

Not by airing your low self-esteem,
hoping someone will come and save you.

CHALLENGE YOUR PERSONS OF INTEREST

You should challenge your person of interest before making them comfortable in your life.

You should challenge them to see how well they conduct themselves when they are not in your presence, as well as how they handle certain situations that test their loyalty, trust and commitment.

Reason being that your person of interest does not only represent themselves, but you, your family, your organizations and so forth. **No need to bring along an individual who do not represent you, your family and your business well.**

Evaluate Your Persons of Interest Effectively.

Your single friends shouldn't be your source for learning how to secure a successful intimate relationship.

Nor those who are buried in an unhealthy relationship.

The best thing for you to do is, evaluate your persons of interest based on the qualities and characteristics that are of importance to you.

Not your friends, not your family, not what you see on television or on social media, but what is of importance to you.

JUST BECAUSE YOUR FRIENDS OR RELATIVES DON'T LIKE WHO YOU ARE INVOLVED WITH DOESN'T MEAN YOU HAVE TO DISMISS THAT PERSON.

Often times, we allow others to negatively influence our relationships by opening our minds to the negative things they have to say about the person we are involved with. Those people are quick to list all the negative qualities your person of interest possesses. They never point out good qualities in that person, but are quick to dismiss that person because of their negative qualities, and they don't offer to help that person become better.

Certain people may attempt to drive you away from your person of interest because their subconscious mind is filled with negative influences such as hatred, selfishness, jealousy and envy. They could be envious of your smile or just plain heartless because they are trapped in an uncomfortable position.

You should be with someone because that's who you want, not to satisfy the desires and appetite of anyone else. It's not your job to convince anyone to like you or the person you are involved with. Your job is to be in the best interest of yourself and the universe will handle those fueled with toxic energy effectively.

The next time someone fixes their mouth to say anything negative about you or someone you are involved with, do one of the following three things:

1.) Ignore them
2.) Ask them, "What Are You Doing to Help Me or Them?
3.) Tell them, before you fix your mouth to talk about anyone, check yourself at the door, because there's a lot of stuff you can be doing to better yourself right now than to worry about how others are living their life. If your motive isn't to help or encourage the person you are speaking negatively about become better, what's the point of talking?

RELATIONSHIPS SHOULDN'T CAUSE PAIN

You are in a relationship to be HAPPY,
to SMILE, to LAUGH and to MAKE GOOD
MEMORIES.

**Not to constantly be UPSET, to Feel
HURT and to CRY.**

Don't allow a holiday, event or expensive items to spoil your relationship.

One shouldn't have to purchase material things or spend their money frivolously, especially around the holiday season to prove their love for you.

Love isn't measured by the amount of money a person has or how much they spend on you. It's measured by the amount of generosity, compassion, intimacy, time, affection, attention, happiness and effort they invest into you from within them.

Expensive items and places should never be a requirement for someone to prove they love you, especially when those items and places are temporary and only benefit the elite's bank account.

Allow your partner to buy your love and prove their love with true intimacy, kindness, compassion, and respect. The true gifts which can't be bought.

BE MINDFUL OF THOSE WHO WILL TRY TO TAKE YOUR PLACE

There are going to be evil spirits that will attempt to discredit your person of interest so you can turn against them, so they can move in and fill that void.

When you have someone who is worthy, many spirits are going to want what you have and they may do whatever they can to take your place.

It's up to you to become strong minded, spot this energy and handle it accordingly. Failure to do so will serve the person who tried and successfully took your place.

Study Your Partner so that when these spirits come around, you won't have to risk losing your spot.

Don't force someone
to marry you.

One who you barely even know,
just to impress those
who don't matter, with
something that has no
value.

Being loyal in a relationship is more than just
being confidential and keeping your underwear on.

It's elevating the entire relationship.

While in your relationship you should try to incorporate midterm and yearly relationship performance evaluations.

The purpose of the performance evaluation is to examine the nature of the relationship **to ensure it's on track, address issues and concerns, correct them and to determine your strengths so that both parties can continue to grow successfully with one another.**

Relationships are like a sound business, you need to know how well your stocks are doing, and if they are behaving poorly, you need to know how to improve them. Relationships shouldn't be free flowing; they should have a goal. This helps all parties stay on track with the purpose of achieving top and bottom line results.

LOVE IS A HEALING SPIRIT

Most say love hurts when something least
expected happens in a relationship.

Love is created by a spirit and something
spiritually created cannot harm us physically.

Love comes and goes. You can fall in
and out of love with the same person
over and over.

But, **when you fall out of love with that
person, it doesn't mean the marathon is
over or that it's time to move on, it simply
means that you have to tap into your inner
spirit and create new ways of loving that
individual.**

When you become emotionally hurt, it
takes love to heal your inner wounds.
Let your guard down and open yourself
up for love. A spirit that will repair you
emotionally, mentally and spiritually.

We all have experienced heartache before
and the truth is, we cannot control the
behavior of those who have caused us great
pain.

However, we can control how we deal
with those distressing experiences; **we can
either heal and move forward or continue
to allow those experiences to overpower us to
prevent us from experiencing happiness again.**

Although many of us have been hurt and many
of us still are, we cannot expect anyone to love
us without giving love first.

"Give love to receive love so that you can heal
properly."

**If we aren't capable of giving love, we aren't
obligated to receive it.**

Love Repairs. Love Heals. Love is Happiness.

Your Departure Doesn't Necessarily Mean Failure for the Other Person.

They Have Actually Gained Something; another opportunity to develop into someone more amazing than before, for someone else to admire, show off, and to appreciate.

So, the statement, "You will never find anyone like me, who've done all the things I've done for you." doesn't mean that the person missing out on you is taking a loss.

Just because the person who you have devoted yourself to have lost interest in you and walked away, doesn't mean that you are no longer valuable, Because you are.

You may have developed the thought, "I'm not good enough."

You aren't valuable to them and that's perfectly fine. Someday, you may cross paths with someone who will give you what they couldn't.

If you are ever faced with, "You will never find anyone like me," respond by saying, "You are absolutely right; I will attract someone who will be more valuable than you."

Your value isn't determined by other people's perception of you or their actions against you, but what is of importance to you and the principles or standards you hold for yourself.

Be Mindful of Your Departure,
because **if you are gone too long,**
that opportunity may become someone
else's.

You didn't appreciate them when you had them.
You didn't value their time when you had it.

**So, don't cry yourself a river when they attract
someone who appreciate them for who they are**
and who value the time your Ex invests
into them.

You dropped the ball, they picked it up.
Fumble!

Show them some Love when You Have Them,
not when they have already found someone
better because **You Treated Them Wrongly!**

Don't Beg Anyone to Stay
**when they Already had Intentions
of Leaving.**

Let them go, create the space
and make the bed for someone
worthy.

It's not that you can't find a good person,
You don't know how to keep them GOOD while they are in your possession.

Often times we drive our person of interest away by trying to love them the way other people love their partners, which is not how they wish to be loved. "Find out how they wish to be loved and love them that way."

Often times we drive them away by being controlling, treating them as if they are our children, instead of treating them as their loving partner, which oftentimes ruin the good within them. "No one wishes to be controlled, but desires to be free to love and to be loved in return."

Often times we allow our friends and families in on our issues, causing us to no longer be our partner's trustful companion, which causes them to no longer share information with us, no longer be around our friends and loved ones, which eventually drives them away. Anger and frustration usually builds up and they no longer have the desire to share their true emotions and feelings. "Learn to be competent and work matters out amongst each other and become a vault."

Your Ex shouldn't be treated
as an enemy **because they threw
in the towel** after being hurt repeatedly by you.

Rejection doesn't mean you
are being punished. It could
mean that the person isn't worthy
of your valued assets.

It's **UNFAIR** that you've **GIVEN** someone who has **HURT** you repeatedly, chance after chance, and not give one chance to that new person who have done nothing wrong.

Why ruin their spark, courage, or spirit of love?

Is that liability really more important than your newly acquired asset?

What about their efforts of restoring you back to your normal state of being?

Their time, love, dedication and affection?

Why send them off to recreate the cycle of hurt, the cycle you are familiar with?

Hurt people, hurt other hurt people.

But, hurt people also hurt good people.

Especially, when that good person **loses themselves in the process** of trying to help those who are hurt heal when they don't want to heal.

Now, there are two hurt people, I mean broken people. That broken person who was once good, now have to learn to heal and find themselves again.
If they will ever.

A FLOWER IN A BROKEN VASE

Who is going to fill me back up when I empty myself into you?

Exactly!

See, you are a flower in a broken vase — I am water and sunlight

When I shine myself onto you and pour myself into your foundation, I wish to be absorbed in your soil and roots, not released through the masking tape covering the cracks on the sides or through the hole on the bottom of your vase.

I am essential for life and therefore I must be kept.
My nutrients and energy must be sustained, not wasted.

I cannot invest into the, who does not invest into thyself, who does not invest back into me.

It is only when your vase is repaired, that I can pour myself into your existence; watering and giving you light so that you may grow.

So, I shall ask, will you repair your vase so that you could grow ?

Will you repair yourself with love, love of self; sealing the cracks that are preventing me from sustaining my love inside of you?

Or will you just allow me to flow out of your vase as your leaves and petals begin to fall off your stem and you crumble ?

Who is going to fill me back up after emptying myself into you?

Broken People Also Hurt Good People

Before I was able to develop self-discipline, I found that Broken Women were attracted to my character and intelligence until they had gotten undressed. After giving their body to me, they became attracted to my love making that resulted in the development of selfishness in an attempt to withhold me from those who need me. The love I deposited into their existence soon led them to become obsessed and they began losing their mind over it, losing sight of my intelligence, character, dignity, worth, the love I possess and the value they have for themselves. Many of their insecurities from their past resurfaced, causing them to lose focus on the future. They have damaged their vision and the foundation that was created. Soon, after experiencing their unwelcomed behavior, I went ghost; un-magically disappearing to a place where I was re-aligned with the universe, my spirit and purpose. While in my place of peace, many had attempted to assassinate my character, sabotage my career, destroyed my properties, caused and attempted to cause physical and psychological harm against me.

Seconds, minutes, hours, days, weeks, and even months go by and while they were drenched in anger, rage, sorrow and regret, they found that my inner flame was glowing brighter than they were used to seeing. They noticed that I had attracted more women to my light as a result of the Elevated Waves that I emit. After witnessing these new women navigate to my light, many have made an attempt to return and it was too late. The problem is, a new pack of broken women have surfaced; covered in foundation that temporary covers the darkness from their past as if they are pure. If I were to pursue either of them, the foundation covering their darkness would smear onto the sheets after a night of pleasure repeating the cycle.

I've become stingy with my intimate and sexual side, as well as my time until I know a woman is worth my complete investment; she have healed from her past bad experiences with other men/women, she value self, children, other women and other men. I almost lost my life because of the time, love, intimacy, respect and loyalty I've invested into broken women. I'm on reserve for a black woman who is complete within. No more broken women for me, but I will continue to uplift them in efforts of preparing them for themselves.

A broken person is a liability to a good person. A Good woman shouldn't nurture a broken man as she would do her children and invite him into her bedroom. He's still a child in an old body. **A Good man shouldn't repair a broken woman while simultaneously massaging her womb with his man part and offering her the title of his woman**; because she would only be absorbing the good out of him without the intentions of sustainability and without knowledge of restoring his electrolytes.

Dating is a beast and I know a vast majority of people aim to heal others during the dating phase. But the truth is, we can't heal anyone who doesn't want to heal. The best thing we can do is prepare ourselves to receive someone worthy and wish great things on those who are damaged.

Broken people do not belong to anyone and shouldn't be focused on building a relationship until they have been fully repaired. The first order of business is finding themselves and their purpose. Complete people who have knowledge of self, their purpose and who are headed to their destination can't share a path with someone who is unsure of whom they are and the direction they are headed in; because that broken person will knock them off their path.

EMOTIONS AND WEAKNESS

Airing your "Single" emotions
on social media is a sign of weakness.

**No strong, successful man or woman,
will claim you as theirs, who lack emotional intelligence.**

Wear your confidence first, even if you
are experiencing emotional distress.

It's okay!

Someday, someone is going to love all the things that make up you. They will listen to all the things you will speak about; they will read your books, sing your songs and even rub your back. They will do all the things those in your past have ignored and have failed to do. You will be happy.

But, you must prepare yourself for that person by developing self-dignity and respect. Carrying yourself unpleasantly will not attract someone great.

However, **when you do find that person, those who have failed, you may be knocking on your door asking for sugar.**

Kindly tell them you are all out.

Interest was expressed,
interest was rejected.

A booty call was expected,
corny I can't mess with.

Success, you made it,
your light they crave it.

You are the basket,
but if I shoot my shot, **it is your responsibility to move
so the ball can go in.**
I'm not forcing a shot that is not there.

05

~~ROMANTIC~~ AFRANTIC

"The art of expressing love and affection among
african descendant couples in an afrocentric way."

I created the word Afrantic (Af-ran-tic) and
Afronce (Af-ran-ce) to represent our original way of
expressing love and affection for one another. We as a
people have adopted the Roman/Greeks words and
ways of expressing love and affection, Romance (Ro-
man-ce) and Romantic (Ro-man-tic), Cupid, teddy
bears, chocolate covered strawberries and Hallmark
Cards that aren't our original words. If you break up
the word romantic, you will have rom-antics, which
are false paradigms of love and affection for the
original man and woman.

Making Love is not the both of us getting naked.

Can You Make Love to Me?

Intimacy doesn't Involve Touch.

Be Intimate with Me.

No, Not Even A Kiss!

Can you Feel the Magic in my Lips from the very same spot on the Coffee Mug where I Placed my Lips to Sip?

That's Love , a Connection, Intimacy, that's a Climax

I'm that guy your grandmother
didn't warn you about,
but the guy she should have suggested
for you **to grab
hold of and to hold onto.**

I see a place deep inside you,
where my spirit of love belongs.

Allow me to **deposit my soul** into
your existence.

My feet cannot be walked on,
but they can be walked next to
if your mind is right and if **you
are willing to put in the necessary
work to help us both walk on the
right path and succeed together.**

LOVE IS...

LOVE IS NOT in the diamond of a ring,
but in the center of your heart.

LOVE IS NOT made of metal, diamonds
or a glossy finish, but of the energy of the
creator within you.

LOVE IS NOT PURCHASED from a jeweler,
but purchased from your core, your spirit.

A wise man long, long, ago once picked an apple from a tree
and proposed to his wife who gladly accepted.

"THE CARROT"

Moments before she told him "Yes," she was figuring out different possibilities to get inside the four chambered organ right beneath my chest.

But that ring, that ring was all that she could see.
Blinded by that material thing;

"He had bashed his ex's face, repeatedly.
Choking her, punching her in the stomach, killing the princess to be."

But somehow, his ex-escaped his physical trap and became silent for the fear of death but, she's forever mentally entrapped.

"New Fiancé," she doesn't know that. She doesn't know that she could be next, or that she is next if he sees a message from me with an emoji hearts face text.

"Girl, he loves me, he just proposed to me." 'This is my chance to be, he really wants me.'

Here is my ring he just bought me. I said, she said, "He Just Bought Me."
Sold into a dream by a shiny thing with karats that aren't even orange and that doesn't mean a thing.

Deep inside her cavity, she's still in search of me;
the powerful plant that heals wounds, I am her sugar, but I fill her cavities.

I am the carrot that detoxifies her system, maintains her beauty and existence, but every Kiss Begins with "K" told her to dismiss me.

But She said "Yes."

"Yes" for the left handed bling to a mysterious soul with no intentions
of depositing himself into her dreams;
but into her face to bruise, into her mind to control,
to confuse, and into her soul to cruise.

To cruise on the abuse, with power; installing fear and providing gifts for
forgiveness with the intent to misuse... again.

I am not a ring, I don't live in a circle, I shine without light, without fame,
I don't cost, I am free. I am the carrot of life,

**I can be found in the garden, not at a jeweler that stole
from African Kings.**

I don't harm, I heal, I Love, I am she, she is me.

I AM HER CARROT!!

UNVEIL YOURSELF, THIS IS YOUR KINGDOM

A filter isn't needed when you are with me.
I accept you for who you are on the inside, not
what's on a photograph.

I can help you unveil your buried treasures so that
you can take your rightful place in your kingdom.

You will no longer have to hide behind photographs, you
can express yourself freely. I can help free your thoughts
and stimulate your mind so that your vision can be
clearer to see the path that is paved right for you ahead.

You are more than just a few likes, comments and shares.

**I see a place deep inside you, where my spirit of love
belongs. Allow me to deposit my soul into your existence.**
I can like, comment and share your desires, and destinies
in my world.

You don't need likes and hearts under your image in order
to feel loved, wanted and needed.

Allow me to turn you inside out, revealing the true ingredients
that makes you appealing, wanted, and desired.

Allow me to grow and maintain your ingredients so we can
feast on your produce. For it will give the world nutrients
needed to survive in your Kingdom.

DEAR QUEEN,

I just want to explore your intellect;
awaken your unconsciousness and
feed your subconscious mind with
the wisdom deep inside me. So that
you can have available the clarity of
life.

I want to help you define your worth,
to show you that you are worth more
than just a sex symbol.

While exploring your wellbeing, you
will understand **it's no longer about
me, it's not about you, it's about us;
achieving all that we can be.** While
adding value to those we encounter
daily and continuously. Developing
Oneness.

I'm not influenced by society's thoughts,
decisions or actions. However, I'm influenced
by the Divine Power I have inside, my inner
God.

I don't follow the norm, it's impossible for me
to lead that way.

So, with your time, attention, love, and affection,
we'd be able to move mountains and experience
the joys of life.

I Discovered a Butterfly in Alaska.

A butterfly later identified as an arctic butterfly, which can be found on mountaintops, over the horizon and everywhere in between.

She is free. Watch her fly.

Watch her rise. Watch her soar across the sea, along with the breeze through the trees.

Arctic chills, with passionate touches.

That tingle to the bone feel.

Captivated by her inner flame and bright comforting wings, those which she uses to glide freely over the Bering Strait waves, keeping my spirit at ease.

Please do not touch her wings. She is free.

I belong In Between Them and they belong around me.

Fly Butterfly Fly. Be all that you can be.

When it's time to rest, here I am, where you will be warm, safe and at peace.

COULD IT BE

She is amazing, I wonder what's next.
I'm not thinking about sex, that's far from next.
That's last on my list, her sexy lips are what I want
to kiss.

I want to stroll with her through the park and flood
her mind with Afrantic thoughts.

Take her smile and make it brighter, get the load off
her back to make her trip lighter.

Have her heart singing songs with no words, take her
love to the top like the birds.

Images of me floating through mind, sitting on the sofa
enjoying a glass of wine.

Turn lust into love, hug tight like a glove.

Keeping her close but not too near, keeping her away but
not too far.

Educate her like a teacher; listen to her like a preacher.
Solve her problems like a puzzle, keep her secrets quiet
like a dog with a muzzle.

Treat her like my best-friend, protect her from the enemies.

Carry her like a queen. pocket her like a penny.

Be the man of her dreams, love her for her and not just what's in her jeans.

Hold her every night; wake up to her every morning.
Kiss her like it's my last, hug her like I don't want to let go.

Show her she's the one that I've been waiting for.

We can walk, we don't have to run.

But if you want to run, run and fall for me, as I run
and fall for you.

Put Your Heart In My Hands,
"I Promise I Will Drop It."

Right Where Mine Belongs.

I WANT TO LOVE YOU

I want to Love you for you, all that you have,
 both inside and out.

**I want to love you, but I don't want to love you
for whom you are pretending to be for the world to see.**

I want to love you, not because you meet my standard,
but because you are giving me all of you; your weaknesses
and strengths.

I want to be your vault; a place where you share your life
and deepest thoughts.

You can be yourself with me.
I want to love you for all you are worth.

**I will not change you, but will cater to your desires
and dreams.** I will help build you up and show you
new things about yourself that will make you more
beautiful and important.

Most importantly, I just want to give you all of me.

My Love is all I have to give.

Before we begin our relationship,
I wish to meet your father.

If he isn't present,
the last man you were under the direction of,
so that I can do what needs to be done.

So that I may reach milestones with you.

I CRAVE YOU

I desire to undress your mind,
caress your consciousness, and
**make the sweetest, sweetest love
to your soul.**

I crave filling your internal chambers
with me, so you can be warm, safe and
at peace.

A SET OF LIPS

So there's these set of lips

A Set of Lips that act as an Electronic Defibrillator when they are joined with mine. These lips send shockwaves through my veins awakening my heart, which then releases a signal to the rest of my body that there's a sign of life.

A life of purpose, spirituality, devotion, selfless, dedication, integrity, hard-work, passion, generosity, empathy, creativity, perseverance, leadership, inspiration and wisdom.

A Set of Lips that are capable of anchoring my mind to a calm, peaceful and relaxing state. **Lips that create a wave of satisfaction every time we meet.** These lips start an intimate connection, better yet, embark on an intimate journey.

Starting with the exterior of my body, puckering around the right side of my neck, heading south, taking its talents down to South Beach.

Puckering on down to my chest, leaving a trail of MAC down my abdomen and into my pelvic region, pausing momentarily...

Proceeding downward inflating my life boat, preparing for a trip to shore, "Miami Beach" and the absorbent of Vitamin D.

Him: My love travels through chambers, out through my arteries, into your veins and into your heart.

Her: My love for you makes me wise, brilliant, and smart; it all started with my heart as it connects with my brain releasing emotional signals I felt from the start.

Him: Those emotional signals you felt, released me through your valves into your lungs, providing you with a fresh breath of life.

Her: With each breath I take, oxygen is consumed with my thoughts of you, carrying you through my bloodstream, exchanging the thought of being your girlfriend with being your wife.

Him: With this fresh breath of life, our love will glide across the mountain tree tops, through the river valleys, and will drip on flannel bed sheets like warm rain drops.

Her: I admire how you hit each spot, allowing tears of love to flow down my cheeks. As our love takes us on this adventurous journey, I vouch to you that this love will never stop.

Him: Slowly traveling deep into your abyss, **I softly stroke your ocean's bottom; I feel you, I fill you up** with all of me. I never wanted you to be my girlfriend; my wife is who you shall be.

Her:

You are truly an amazing person and I look forward to getting to learn more about you and establishing a healthy, natural and fun friendship with you! And we know the rest will fall into place, because this chemistry and vibe is undeniable. It's like we both feel this force of energy and we're doing our best to pace it out- but it's so strong and feels so good.

Just being around you inspires me to do more and see more and feel more. I never want to forget this feeling.

Thank you for existing.
I was really in a dark, dark, DARK place quite some time ago. I was one of the people that said I was numb and that I prayed to be emotionless, because I didn't want to feel pain anymore. I didn't want to ever be "in my feelings" anymore. I hurt so bad back then, so I was just trying to protect myself.

You offering me your friendship, your undivided attention, your time, your patience, your body, your wisdom and your energy makes me change my mind about wanting to be numb. I guess it's a risk that I am willing to take. If I was numb, I wouldn't feel the positive energy and kindness that you've been showering me.

Here's a toast to liking each other!!

Him:

I've been in tunnel vision since we've met and have been focusing on soaking up your vibes and piecing our lives together.

I'd never forget our very first time hanging out together, which was one of the most beautiful intimate experiences I've ever experienced. It was fun; the vibes flowed freely.

I admired you more after learning about your growth, learning that we've traveled similar paths, went a separate route, met back in the middle and have decided to proceed forward together.

Naturally, you were already equipped with each value I require in a woman, but you added your own flavor without me having to instruct you to do anything. You have already exceeded my minimal list of requirements and you excite me more and more each day.

Do you know how hard it is to find a woman of your caliber? It's not easy at all. **I've always envisioned my woman wearing your shoes but I didn't know you would be the one wearing the wedges.**

My duty is to protect you from going back down those dark roads you have traveled before and to be that balance you need.

It's beautiful that we aren't aligned with all commonalities because we wouldn't be able to debate or try anything new.

For me, debating is fun, it challenges and trains the brain and **I can kiss and love on you even after I get you worked up or after you get me worked up. That competitive rage of yours is exciting to watch. Your strength sparks my arousal.**

I spot both good and bad energy before it gets to me and I felt you a mile away. **I feel that you deserve me, have earned me, despite wanting**

to be numb from loving and experiencing hurt from loving again. I know the feeling all too well.

Pain is the fuel needed to achieve our desires. We can't want rock hard abs and give up when we feel the burn. We have to push past the uncomfortable feeling and secure what we desire, which is to feel complete within; to be successful. You didn't give up on you.

I like you and really like you, because you are the opposite of me but at the same time, the same as me. You have an on and off switch like me. You have professional attributes like me, you are a thinker like me, you take on leadership roles like me, you take care of your family like me, you have a sense of humor like me, you are freaky and nasty like me, you show generosity like me. Like me, you want to be in my presence as much as I want to be in yours.

Thank you for being vulnerable and for allowing me to show you how a woman should be appreciated, admired and devoured. I understand you had/have your armor up, which you are supposed to especially from what you have endured. Banks would get robbed all the time without a security system and armed guards.

Today, we toast to the day we rekindled our friendship, officially placing our hands upon another, spending hours exchanging vibes and sacrificing our safety and sleep for wanting to learn and be with each other more. I knew each day forward would grow to a better foundation of friendship and would eventually manifest into something even greater. On the day we re-met, you could have easily gone inside the house after a few minutes or after your glass of wine and I could have gone home if the vibes were off. But they weren't and because they weren't and I've stayed true to my being, we are still able to cherish old memories and create more exciting ones, like visiting the number one amusement park in the country - Welcome Back Rider, How Was Your Ride?

I bit into her and found
she was what I had been missing all along.
I was nourished.

I found my favorite fruit **inside her.**

As your eyelids begin to separate, revealing your pupils to read this message, I would like to welcome you to this beautiful day.

I've been awaiting your arrival.

No Strange Fruit!

You may have once believed your fruit to be strange or sour because of those who have spit you out prior to meeting me. The truth is, your fruit has always been sweet and nourishing.

Those who have come before me taste buds had malfunctioned from all the garbage they've placed in their mouth prior to biting into you.

Your fruit had begun to deteriorate, not because you have been sitting out too long or because you were growing old, but because of the bad taste (broken tongue) in their mouth, filled with bacteria that have gotten inside of you.

I want to inform you that your fruit was never the problem, **as you were the seed planted in the earth who've become the plant created to multiply abundance of fruit to feed me over and over again.**

I have placed my cleansed mouth over your infected areas, preventing the deterioration from spreading.

I have injected my nutrients into your wombs, administering CPR to the nearly dead cells and roots their decomposed mouth have caused. You will go on to live.

No Strange Fruit!

You have always been sweet and oooh you taste sooo good.

No Strange Fruit!

I've eaten all of what you have produced and placed in my mouth, upon my tongue and I am not at all ill.

Keep on feeding me; your fruit is not strange.

No Strange Fruit!

In you, I did not find myself;
I had already been found!

In you, I found a reason to stay
and love you, to protect you, grow
with you and **to die belonging
only to you.**

I wish to lay my head upon your breasts,
resting my eyes to the peaceful, rhythmic song playing beneath them.
Within minutes, I know I'd be sound asleep.

I crave to be fed your love and restorative energy,
while I'm deep off into my REM, stimulating the regions
of my brain needed for protein development and our cultural
advancement.

**Come morning or when I decide to awake, I crave being nourished
and energized by your love, ready to concur the day; gracefully
honoring and thanking you for goddess powers.**

Your breasts are the antidepressants to my stress, Motrin to my migraines and
Tylenol to my fevers.

You are the medicine to my sickness and pain,
the ingredients and nutrients to my existence.

I crave you.

Your emojis aren't able to speak
and neither can your mind.

Your lips are unsure,
so **I'll listen to your body.**

She whispered to me,
"I'm yours."

06

IN BETWEEN
HER

I promise I can fuck you right...

I know you are anxious for the euphoria this adventure will bring, but I recommend using a sheath before entry.

The riptide could be deadly.

Getting caught without one could cost you your life.

Hey Mama, I need to talk to you about...

"Son, I told you she's a nice girl and that you two would be good for each other. And besides, she goes to church and she loves the lord."

"But Mama..."

"But Mama Nothing!"

"But Mama, that girl is a Freak!"

She put her mouth on my mic and the next thing you know it disappeared and I blanked out.

"OH LAWD HAVE MERCY!
Just like his daddy, Junior. done got himself
A SOUL-SNATCHER."

"I thought she... but she's the lead singer in the church choir.."

"Lord please, protect my boy. Shelter him from the wolf that howls in sheep's clothing at night."

"Mama, when I woke up, I had lost the feeling in my toes and she was right there with my mic in her hand licking her lips, getting ready to pull it towards her mouth like she does the microphone before she begins to sing.

Then, she kissed my mic and slid it in her mouth making it disappear again.

"I SCREAMED"

"She snatched the spirit out of me!"

"Mama, you were right! She is good for me.
Thank you for encouraging me to give her a chance."

Breakfast please!

I want you served as my nutritional shake
and for you to **come balance that tasty pussy
of yours on my tongue like a gymnast.**

My Balanced Diet

It would be heaven on my tongue to have your
crystal waters and diamond juices twerking like
Cardi on my taste buds while you are singing

"Please Me" into my golden Microphone.

If you aren't confident enough to open that pretty
lil mouth of yours and **tell me you want me,**

you will never be able to get it as wet as you
would like to for me.

Have you ever had someone who effortlessly made both sets of your lips blush at once?

Like, made saliva leak out your creases, licking it up, putting it back in your mouth, slurping it all down with joy?

Have you?

Have you ever had someone French Kiss your lips so good that your back forms an arch, locking in the arch position with your legs wedged open, as you flood the sheets and he cover his face with pie?

Have you?

Have you ever felt so good that you tried to break his wedge and stop him and he didn't let you? And he smiled as you struggled to break free?

Have you ever had someone look you in your eyes while devouring you with excitement and you drizzled, frosting all in his mouth? And he licked his lips?

Have you?

Have you ever had someone belch in satisfaction after finishing his tasty treat?

If not, what are you waiting for?

Allow me to make you smile cheek to cheek and thigh to thigh.

How many licks would it take for your thighs to widen?
For your back to lock in the arch position, and for you to
reach for my shaft, guiding me between your dripping lips,
until I reach the center of your pussy and make your pussy pop?

Let's count together...

One wet Sunday afternoon after service, I found her bottomless in her Elevated Waves tank enjoying a glass of my favorite wine in between those sheets of hers; pink silk satin.

Mesmerized by her sexy thighs and soft and lovely lips, **I instantly became aroused and marinated the head of my enlarged, swollen dick inside her glass of Sangria.**

Suddenly,
she slurped it all off... **"Sloppy"**

Engulfing it all.

"ODI"

She said, "She Doesn't Speak French."
But she can Tongue me Down.

Excuse me,
I'm having trouble seeing her;
your panties are in my way.

Can you slide them over just a bit?

Your Presentation is important, but your ingredients have earned you a spot on my face.

Take a seat, my tongue will be right in you.

Have you nutted all on a poet's mouth
as he **spoke stanzas into your pussy** like he delivered
his award-winning piece when he won?

I kinda figured you really hadn't had your pussy eaten.

You just been nibbled on, huh?

I would like to invite you to my Open Mic night

"I just love how both sets of your lips form saliva and work collaboratively to show their appreciation for me by French kissing me softly and with passion.

"Go Best Friend, Suck that Dick. Go Best Friend, Swallow that Shit."

You can uncross your legs, I have flood insurance. Just allow your juices to flow until I fix the leak."

I gracefully desire to be wrapped passionately in your body;
indulging in your edible pink, wet, warm and soft sponge.

I wish to allow you to absorb me freely, squeezing me tighter and tighter,
as you begin to secrete more and more, **and more of your delicious
juices**, with each thrusting stroke until we climax together.

You can say what you won't do, but your body will disagree with you and side with me.

You are no longer in control!

Your body wants me and me is who your body will have.

Your mind is locked in one place, but your body is thinking about me freaking it in other places like in your boss's office, reacting in ways your mind can't fathom.

What you are saying is running off my skin like your vagina's lubrication running down your legs.

I can't hear you!

See, your mind doesn't want me, but your body does and your body's desire
shall be granted.

Your words will be silenced, and your lips will be sealed by the wet, gentle touch of my lips.

Breathe!

Your mind no longer has control of your body and your body never really belonged to you.

I have set your body free from you. With me is where it should be.

I'm in control of your fingers and I will have them finger spell, "don't stop" on my back, as your other hand slowly submerge my submarine into your sea. Telekinesis!

I have control over your body, but you are free; free to come and go as you please.

My playground is where your mind and body will soon want to stay, with or without you being naked.

No Treasure Map, but X mark the spot

Diving onto your pillow-top mattress,
swimming **In Between Your Sheets.**

Slowly separating your **Thick and
Curvy** thighs, finding a pair of
sealed warm tender lips that are
gatekeepers for your buried treasure.

Passionate and gentle knocks at your entrance,
igniting shock waves throughout your body, defusing
your body's control center to allow me inside.

Lick once, Lick twice, Suckling all on your Pearl.
Struck Gold, Gems.

Lips, whole **tongue buried** in your treasure chest.

Lucky Charms.

Royal Rich Tongue.

Golden Dick.

Leprechaun Under Your Sheets!

Heist

Listen very, very carefully!

This is a heist!

Do not scream! And you better not try to run!

Turn off your cellular phone and hand it over!

Sit down on the bed and slowly remove your shoes and all articles of your clothing.

Place this purple blindfold over your eyes and I better not catch you peeking!

Lay back on to the bed and slowly turn over your stomach planting your face into the sheets.

Grip the sheets with both hands, and gradually toot your bottom upward until an arch is formed and your lower back is locked into place.

Perfect! Stay just like that!

Do not move!

I am going to gently insert my tongue, followed by my erect dick into you.

Unlock your treasure chest.

I want you to empty all of your contents into my mouth and onto my thrusting dick.

You understand? Good!

Hey! Shhh!

Listen, Bite that pillow!

BINGO! There it is!

This treasure is all mine!

Drown Me in A Pool of Your Pleasure...

If All the Raindrops Were Juices from Your Juice Box

If all the raindrops
were juices from your juice box
oh what a facial that would be
Sitting under that pussy with my mouth open wide,
Ah, ah, ah, ah, ah, ah, ah, ah, ah, ah

If all the raindrops
were juices from your juice box
oh what a facial that would be

"I can get working on that"
"Oh, look at that"
"I hope you keep on squirting"
"Oh, cum on my face"

If all the snowflakes
tasted like your cupcake
Oh what blizzard it would be
licking all the icing with your thighs open wide,
lap, lap, lap, lap, lap, lap, lap, lap, lap, lap,

If all the snowflakes
tasted like your cupcake
Oh what blizzard it would be

"I'd be outside all day"

ECSTASY

Exploring that water, wet, wetness,
deep inside that membrane;
diving, gliding, stroking, floating, treading as you drip, drop, squirt, flow,
soak my mind with a climax of no return.

Upon your request, your demand will be delivered;
shipped on a yacht, cruising to your desired acceleration.

Surfing your waves, back peddling in your ocean current,
submerged so deep, scuba-divers can't bring me back to surface.

Moments later, I rise to surface, drenched in your love, I drowned on
purpose.

Two minutes of Mouth to Mouth after being lost at sea,
cardiac arrest, thirty more compressions, can you feel my heartbeat?

Extracting our bottoms:
her pink panties, my draws.

Silver bullet at a frequency of 89 Hz,
shaking sweet juices out of her walls.

Splash, Splash, Gush, Gush,
squirming around in her seat:
Lips touching, body rubbing, sensations
so exciting and unique.

Pussy throbbing, Dick gliding, Dick sliding so deep:
Bodies shaking, juices flowing, an earthquake is forming beneath.

Muscles contracting, lip biting, she erupted all on me.
She sat me up, put it down; I wasn't trying to get free.

She took me to her spot, that favorite spot I love to be;
Up and down, back and forth, twirling around all on me.

Slipped in the cut, time for a nut,
my volcano exploded uncontrollably.

I know you don't want anybody near your beautiful canvas but me;

I know you don't want nobody slobbering on that pussy, licking and suckling all on those lips but me.

I know you don't want nobody drenching those panties, trickling your juices down your thighs and licking it all up but me.

I know you don't want to firmly grasp those oozing walls around and climax all over nobody but me.

So, allow me to make you feel right.

So your pussy has insomnia?

While you are resting, she's up moving around,
trying to peep and creep out of those panties and
sheets for me?

I know just what to do...

Look, tonight after I lay you to bed, **I'll be singing lullabies
to my pussy until she's sound asleep**, drifting off into
the stars.

Sweet Dreams My Love!

SIP and PAINT

I'm in no race or competition to prove which of us can serve you better. I'm just here to let you know my touch is strictly reserved for me.

See, sex is a form of art and I am a Gestural Abstraction and Graffiti Artist. I am the brush to your canvas and the spray paint to your river mural.

Once I insert my brush into your palette of paint, my only desire is to complete your portrait; spontaneously dribbling, splashing and smearing your paint, while gliding my body onto your canvas until satisfaction have been reached.

I'm not here to just wet my brush.

This spray can of mine will turn your walls into breathtaking waterfalls that you would often want to visit like Niagara.

See, not only is the touch of my brush magical, so is my timing and affection.

As you enjoy the thrill of me being with and inside you, I'm checking your vitals to breath at the same rate as you, to gasp and moan with you.

During our breathing intervals, I love to passionately lick, suck and kiss all on your sternocleidomastoid, breasts and lips along with each stroke of my brush as you begin to lose control and erupt.

While you are covering me with your April showers, I'm looking at you with excitement, deeply into your eyes, smiling at your expressions of satisfaction.

Wow! Look at my work

You are my canvas and at this point, you are secured on my easel; no getting free.

The strokes of my brush will begin to flow more rapidly than before, increasing the rate of our simultaneously beating hearts. Our synch gasps and moans will become more and more intense, as I time your next eruption to erupt with you, creating a very valuable work of art.

Love has been made. Can you afford me?

Auctioneer, you may start the bid.

You dipped my brush into your cup of water,
then into your palette of paint and began softly
stroking the bristles onto your blank canvas.

You turned your dry canvas into magical waterfalls
as you submerged my brush deeper into your sparkling blue.

A river flowed so freely in the horizon.

Your canvas wasn't secured on my easel, but my easel
was secured on you. You kept me near until you released
your grip and at that moment, I knew your portrait was complete.

THE GRAND OPENING

He fathered your child(ren) without you being able to nut all in his mouth, on his penis and without your warm juices flowing down his balls as he promised you would.

"What A Selfish Dick!"

"An Unfulfilled Fantasy"

Hey, hey; look at me!

I know it's unfair and I am sorry that you couldn't celebrate the release of your pineapple juices with your friends during ladies' night.

"She begins to cry"

Hey, don't cry. It's ok!

I'll throw you a ribbon cutting ceremony and we can cut the ribbon right off of those Black Lace Vicky Panties together and give you a proper grand opening.

"Wait! How Do You Know What I Have On?"

When you stretched your torso, your shirt rolled up and revealed the red ribbon on the top of your panties.

Look, put his kid(s) in bed and meet me in the kitchen over by the stove.

"Wow, she looks Amazing!"

"I can only imagine how beautiful her pussy looks and how good it would feel to have her clitoris gliding back and forth on my soft wet mouth until her warm frosting stains my tongue."

"I bet she have it trimmed fine and shaped like the top of a martini glass."
"Oooh, a Dirty Martini with Pineapple on the Rocks."

Have a seat on the counter by the butter rolls.

I have a craving for something sweet; your tropical treat beneath that purple silk robe.

"A Purple Robe?"

Wait! How did she know?

"Holy Waters!"
Take Me to Her Fountain of Youth!

"She can dip and bathe my whole face in it!"

"Once I get going, drinking from her Spring, I ain't stopping until I am full and her well has run dry."

Suckle on my bottom lip if you grant me permission to take full control of this ceremony and permission to turn on your phone's camera and record this groundbreaking moment.

Instead of sharing a story neither of your friends is going to believe, I want you to show them this video of you celebrating the grand release of your pineapple juices.

Welcome to the Grand Opening and Ribbon Cutting Ceremony for your Pineapple Juice Bar.

Before I indulge into you and begin my liquid fast, allow me to bless you and the main ingredient in the smoothie that has been prepared for me;

Dear Pineapple,

Bless Me, oh Bless Me with your vitamins and nutrients which I am about to receive from your roots, which will soon be blasted down my esophagus. I apologize for you not being cared for, kissed on, licked on, sucked on, swallowed and digested properly.

"Thank you Creator for not allowing her baby daddy's weak, selfish mouth and dick be able to make her cum."

"I'm about to be the one to give her the thrill of her life."

"Her friends are about to be Jealous, Jealous."

You will soon be able to produce gallons of your juice after my tongue begins to vibrate on your juicy flesh.

Thank you for your love and flavor.

Bless my tongue and this countertop we pray, Amen!

Relax, I'll grab you a bib. I know she's about to be spitting up soon.

Watch me closely, as I begin to slowly separate your trembling thighs from each other and peel off your drenched panties from your pretty warm damped vagina.

"Damn, she's wet! The tips of my fingers are moist."

"I'm about to suck it all off and see how she reacts."

"Oooh she's spitting up! Look at it race down her thighs!"

Don't be alarmed, these gold plated ribbon cutting scissors are for us to cut the ribbon. Remember, this red one holding these together?

You take the right side and I'll take the left.

On your count of three, we will cut the ribbon, smile for your camera and open the doors to your juice bar.

"On five, I'm taking those scissors, cutting open her Vicky's
and planting my mouth right on her fountain."
One, Two, Three!

"Four and Five!"

"Lap Lap Lap Lap Lap"

"I got myself all thirsty and shit by getting her all anxious and ready.
I hope she have enough to quench my thirst."

"Damn! He let all of this go to waste?
Shit, I'll take it!

"I hope she has flood insurance, because it's finna be a hurricane in this kitchen..."

Ladies night is this Friday, right?

Go on, enjoy yourself and celebrate with your friends.
Tell me all about it later.

"Hey y'all, I finally got my kitty tamed"

"Girl, I'm surprised his mouth isn't numb and he ain't dead from me waterboarding him. Their daddy has never eaten my pussy that good. I came all over my kitchen counter and he slurped it all up like an ICEE.

"And His Dick. It's Amazing!
"I think my kids may have a new daddy."

"I have never heard of or met a man who can cum back to back, to back. I thought y'all said only women can do that and when a man cum, that's it?"

"His dick is magical! I kissed, licked and sucked all on it, for making me cum sooo many times. After he came, he started fucking me again. I had to kick his ass off me."

"Shut your lying, no good dick getting ass up Keisha. Out the blue your ass pop up with a man with a golden dick! Bullshit!"

"Y'all wanna see?"

Can I FaceTime that pussy later?

I would like to personally let her know
how good she made me feel this morning
and how much she means to me.

She was fun...

Satisfying your sexual appetite is healthy.
Not doing so is unhealthy.

Sex is natural; it's what makes us who we are
and it helps us in many different ways.

Doing what the rest of the world says is right
isn't always the best route to take.

Part of being an adult and owner of self is
expressing yourself fully and feeding your desires.

If you haven't been satisfied sexually,
you have every right to be sexually satisfied as long
as it's not in violation of the human rights of another
human being.

If you want him to catch that drip, let him.

If he wants his lightening rod to be massaged by you and you
want to massage it, massage it.

Neither he nor you need anyone else's approval.

07

WATERING
THE *SEEDS*

SANTA

"Before lying to your children about why Santa didn't bring them the gifts they asked him for, **Just Tell The Truth."**

One of the worst things you can do as a parent or as an adult is lie to Children. Tell them the truth about old Saint Nicholas, his reindeer, elf's and your bank account balance.

It's terribly wrong for you to use their behavior as an excuse for you not being able to afford what they have requested for Christmas.

Let's put an end to the tradition of lying to our children about Christmas and educate them on the true meaning of Christmas. Also, let's stop spending all of our money on gifts that have no real value, leaving us flat broke. Christmas is every day.

STOP EXPECTING THEM TO ACT LIKE AN ADULT WHEN THEY AREN'T.

You can't expect a Young Girl to be a mother
when she hasn't been taught how to be one.
Nor can you expect a Young Boy to be a father
when he hasn't been taught how to be one.

You can't expect a Young Girl to love you when
her mother never taught her how to love and
nor can you expect a Young Boy to be responsible,
when his dad never taught him to be a leader.

**Don't expect a Young Girl to perform as a woman
because she's not and don't expect a Young Boy to
take on the role of a man because he is not one.**

Instead of expecting them to act like an adult,
I encourage you to teach them and show them
how to become one.

THERE'S NO PRIVACY WHEN IT COMES TO PROTECTING YOUR CHILDREN.

Dear Parents and Guardians,

It's very important that you take time out to really know your children. Learn their attitudes when they're upset, hurt, afraid, as well as when they're happy. It's even more important that you know who their friends are. Store their friend's number in your phone or contact book. Be sure to develop a positive relationship with their friend's parents and save their contact information as well. Be mindful of what they post on social media sites such as Facebook, Instagram and Twitter and who they interact with on those sites. Always be aware of their whereabouts; especially their place of employment and the extracurricular programs they are part of. "There's No Privacy When It Comes To Protecting Your Children."

I say this because, suppose you go to pick up your daughter at her job, and found out she have never worked there?

Imagine you arrive at the restaurant where she told you she worked and you call her cell numerous times to come outside and you got no answer. You think to yourself that, maybe she's staying late for overtime, and you decide to head back home. It's now midnight and she isn't home. She hasn't called you. Maybe she went to her friend's house after work and she will come in a little later, you say to yourself. You fall asleep awaiting her return home. It's now morning and you found that she hasn't come home and you have no missed calls from her. You try calling her and you got no answer. You try again and again, but still no answer. You phone the police and file a missing person's report and you notify everyone in your address book and inform them that your daughter is missing. **You are worried sick. You head back to the restaurant where she works, enter and show the manager the picture of your missing daughter and asks if he has seen your daughter. The manager replies, "I've never seen her before, are you sure she works here?"** You ask the other employees and you get the same response. You head out to the door to the restaurant, totally confused. Your daughter told you that she works here, and they're telling you that she doesn't.

Her picture has been posted across the city and not a soul has provided you information regarding your daughter's disappearance. Weeks have passed and you haven't heard from or seen your little girl.

You receive an unexpected call from the detective stating that your daughter has been found. You find out that the restaurant that she supposedly worked at ran a human trafficking operation, bringing people into the country, farming them out as slave labor. Taking all their rights away, turning them into prostitutes and beating them when they disobey and when they try to run away. Your daughter was caught up in the operation. All the employees of the restaurant have been coached to say they have not seen your daughter to cover up the human trafficking operation they were running there.

On the day of her disappearance, she witnessed an Asian girl being tied up and being forced to perform oral sex on some guys running the operation. She also witnessed a child being beaten with a stick by an older

Caucasian woman for trying to run away. Your daughter was surprised at what she had seen and screamed. Her loud scream caught the attention of the guys and she tried to run away. One of the guys caught her and brought her back to the room where the mistreatment was taking place. She was forced into the human trafficking operation ran at the restaurant.

Somehow, one of the trafficked girls managed to escape and notified authorities of the operation that was being ran at the restaurant. Upon rescue of the trafficked persons, you've learned that she had been working 18 hours a day for little to no pay. She has been mentally, emotionally, sexually and physically abused and she had been given a new name. Her pride was shot, she was filled with fear and her smile was ripped away from her face. She was damaged. Your Happy Little Girl Was Gone.

DEAR CHILDREN,

There are people out here who will mistreat you and hate you because of the color of your skin, your hair, the clothes and shoes you wear, your economic and social status, etc.

When you come in contact with them, I want you to remain humble and walk away with your head held high. If you fall into their trap, they can potentially destroy who you are.

Stay focus on the goal.

There's no need to discipline (abuse) your child (ren) when you or the people they spend the most time around have no discipline. Their actions are a result of the behavior of their environment.

Kids mimic behavior and if they aren't presented something different such as a healthy and loving environment, they will continue to mimic the poor behavior of their environment.

Chemical behavior, as well as generational curses such as whooping's/ beatings, won't correct their behavior either. If anything, it makes it worse especially if the parent(s) aren't knowledgeable of the problem at hand.

You shouldn't whoop or discipline a child, especially if no one is whooping you for your poor behavior, in which they may have got it from, is all I'm saying.

Disciplined parents are parents who are knowledgeable of self, their behaviors and are taking control of their own behaviors, while taking appropriate measures so that their children receive proper treatment.

Before disciplining your child, ground yourself (take control of yourself), then **determine what the cause of the behavior is and correct it. Love them after and praise them when they do things right on their own.** Resorting to just whooping's isn't going to correct the situation and help your child grow up to become successful and responsible adults.

Stop forcing your kids to become mis-educated in a school system that is not designed for them to be great. Keep your hands off of them!

Why are you whooping and/or beating your child, in order to make them cooperate in a classroom with an instructor who is preparing them to fail?

"Never let the ones who've enslaved you, teach you about anything. Because they are only going to teach you what they want you to know. Even in Religion."
— Dr. Ben Carson

A few months ago, a black mother posted on social media about her son's behavior in school and requested advice from her followers on what to do to correct his behavior. Many responded by saying, "Whoop his Ass."

"We watched our slave owners and slave capturers beat us with whips and other objects, now we beat each other, our children with similar objects just as we have been beaten to honor those who are truly against us. Oppression!

What will happen is that your children will grow to believe that violence is the solution to solving problems.

While many were all for the woman's son to receive a spanking, I was against it. I told the mother, the school he attends could be a major factor in his behavior; it may not necessarily be him. Most educational institutions do not meet the needs of the students, but rather make the students tend to their needs of making their job easier, which is not right, because the students are the reason they are employed.

When most of us learn, we don't learn what works best for us, but what works best for our teachers. Black males as well as females aren't going to be receptive to educators who aren't able to resonate with them. Each student has different learning styles, which means that there has to be a different approach, especially one that inspires them to behave and learn. Most teachers only teach one way and expect every student to grasp everything taught in that style of teaching.

A black child, who learns differently with the style that is being used to teach, especially by a teacher who doesn't look like them, is said to have a learning disability or behavior problem because they aren't receptive to the information being presented. Their parents are called and informed that their child have been misbehaving and wasn't paying attention in class. During the call, the teacher failed to inform the parent(s) that they only teach lecture style to their child who is a visual learner, and in the midst of them not being able to grasp the information, the child sought attention elsewhere. The child is then disciplined severely by their parent(s).
I told the boys mom,

"No one could force me to be still in a classroom, with an instructor teaching me something I'm not inspired by, in her own style of teaching that makes it convenient for her and difficult for me. I'm going to focus my attention elsewhere."

Another reason boys may act out in school is because boys have a lot of testosterone, which gives us a lot of energy, making them active. Many have to burn that energy off and sitting in a classroom where energy can't escape is going to drive many of them crazy. That is not how most of us learn. By nature, we learn by doing, by being active. Not sitting still.

So, don't beat him as many have suggested, but instead, evaluate the teaching style of the teachers without them knowing you are evaluating them if you can, because many of them hide their true self when parents are present in their classroom.

If the problem happens to be your son, identify and correct the problem without violence and without instilling fear. Correct, Love and praise them. If the problem is indeed the school and the educator, have your child moved to a more feasible learning environment.

It has been reported that, kids of color who don't sit still or behave in class, are told to have ADHD by teachers who have no education or training in psychology. They inform parents that their child must see a psychiatrist.

"Never let the ones who've enslaved you, teach you about anything..."

Many parents of color go and have their child checked out by a psychiatrist, who confirms that their child do have ADHD and prescribe them medication that forces them to sit still in class. Many parents fail to seek a second or third opinion from another psychiatrist and allow their child to be hooked on Crack Cocaine, which is said to have been found in the medication to treat ADHD. The medication is said to help with coping skills while in school. When the meds don't work, parents conform to punishing their children by the way of whippings and beatings.

As a suggestion, schools especially intercity schools should try incorporate gym in the morning, as opposed to the afternoon, so that boys and girls who are very active can burn off their energy early and not later. This may help them be calm during class time. Also, they would have built up enough energy after school to do homework, as opposed to being tired and restless from participating in gym in the afternoon. They also would be energized the next morning, preparing to have fun in gym and engaging in classroom activities.

I remember growing up; I had to attend several different elementary schools. Every school I attended caused problems: I was forced to lose friends, meet new friends, fight students who didn't accept me and conform to teaching styles of teachers who wasn't passionate about teaching but working for a paycheck.

Have you taken a moment to realize that many of your educational instructors are in the same classroom teaching the same stuff long after you have left? The same teachers that have encouraged you to graduate college, but is in debt up to the ceiling? The same teachers who obtained their degree and wasn't able to work in the school district of their choice, so they lost their passion for education, haven't acquired new knowledge or technology, so they do/did enough just to receive a paycheck?

Have you taken a moment to think that many of us enter an institution debt free and leave buried in debt, not being able to become financially wealthy or to secure the job we were promised?

I learned that, having Straight A's and B's from outdated curriculum and textbooks from Kindergarten through college serve no real purpose in life and that the only report card that matters is your Financial Statement. No one ask or even care if you got perfect attendance or honor roll in the fourth grade. Employers don't ask about the grades you received in your freshman year of college electives. I believe schools are designed to program us to become professional employees from the time we enter grade school to securing our first job. They don't teach real life skills, just job skills. They teach us how to manage the daily oppressions of someone else's dream and nothing about ours. Becoming someone's doctor, lawyer, dentist, teacher or police officer is a job, not a Dream.

So, why continue to force our children to go through the same revolving door with the hopes of them doing it better than us? It will never work!

For most, a College Degree is a certificate of debt owed to the federal government that takes a decade or more to pay off, which postpone you from living the life you desire. Most CEOs and business owners do not have a college degree. We are now in the "Do it Yourself" era, the information era where you can do it without a formal Euro-American education. Your child shouldn't have to spend eight or more hours in school and come home to do homework for the rest of the day. You are taking away from their childhood and distracting them from their purpose. Use the time at home to allow them to be kids, as well as to prepare them for real world experiences.

So parents, please stop forcing your kids to become miseducated in a school system that is not designed for them to be great.

Your child shouldn't have to spend eight
or more hours in school and come home to
do homework for the rest of the day.

You are taking away from their childhood
and distracting them from their purpose.

**Use the time at home to allow them to be kids,
as well as to prepare them for real world experiences.**

Set your child free so they can fly.

Little Brothers and Sisters,

Don't be upset because you didn't receive a certificate of merit or honor, success is what you say it is, not what anyone else say it is. It's definitely not limited to what grades you receive in school. You can print off your own certificates or buy them at Dollar Tree.

C-Average students are my favorite people and in fact, they are the most accomplished people in the world because they don't just focus on academics, information geared towards making their employers dreams come true, but on information to make their own dreams come true.

A 4.0 GPA means nothing if your education isn't equivalent to the other surrounding school districts. A 4.0 at Berea High School here in Ohio isn't the same as a 4.0 at East Tech High School. There's a huge gap.

I recall graduating from South High School, being the only recipient of an Honors Diploma and **I wasn't fortunate enough to receive a full ride scholarship to college.** After graduating from college, I realized that I was in a trap and made it my duty to escape immediately.

Brothers and Sisters, these academic awards do not determine your worth nor your future, you do.

Anyone can print off a certificate and sign it. Who's really going to call your Second-Grade teacher and verify that you really had citizenship?

#StopMiseducatingOurYouth

I remember studying Human Evolution at Kent State University and my professor was all for Darwin's Theory of Evolution and I was against it.

So, since I was against it and my arguments and research papers were cited properly, I barely passed. Lol

To those who are studying certain information behind people that hold academic accredited titles, just because they have that title doesn't mean the information they present is accurate.

Don't be afraid to challenge those who take on the role of education. **We have history teachers teaching people of African descent that our history began in slavery.** That is false.

Don't Give Them All the Answers,
Because You Would Be Teaching Them
What to Think, Not How to Think.

The objective of life is for us to learn how to think on our own,
so that our goals and dreams are ours and not anyone else's.
Also, so that we are able to make sound decisions on our own.

In the mist of achieving our objectives, we must carry ourselves
with great character, dignity and respect, and take the pledge to
become a student for the rest of our life.

This is how our children will honor us and how our legacy will
carry on.

I believe one of the worse things you can do as a parent,
**is force your child to live their life based on the vision
you have for them.**

They have their own mind and set of eyes for a reason.

Prepare them to attract whatever it is they envision for themselves,
not what you want. It's their life, not yours.

**BEING REAL,
MEANS TELLING THE TRUTH
DESPITE HOW THE LISTENER MAY REACT
OR FEEL**

08

TURN ON THE LIGHTS

" You will never be able to shine if you are always hiding in the Dark. Darkness doesn't shine in the Light, Light shines in Darkness"

The Truth Isn't Always Pretty.
That's Why It's Said, "The Truth Hurts"

WHITE

I use to know white as being just a color;
like the color of milk and fresh snow during winter.
Like white cotton, rice and sugar;
picked by brown hands that formed blisters and splinters.
Like white paper used in printers.

Now, I see white clowns
painted the bronze glowing like feet
pale white so we can forever bow to their feet.
While they paint their face brown, juggle our life around,
laugh at the fact that we are inferior to them and still haven't been
found.

I use to think white symbolized peace like heaven and clouds, white gowns,
you know the kind worn at weddings?

Now I see white clowns dressed in white gowns,
imitating white Jesus in the sanctuary and on mosque grounds.
White evil spirits shaped in the form of man, brainwashing the minds of
the masses,
telling you to put all your faith in man,
the white-man, white Jesus.

Cesare Borgia to be exact;
a pale white roman who has a satanic connection, and that's a fact.
It's okay if you are dumb-founded, I didn't know either.
The truth has been revealed, no need to celebrate Easter.

I use to like white until it was no longer just a color,
until it was joined with man to create an evil empire, "oppression,"
to keep my people under.

Now, I can't even use white and man
together in the same sentence,
you know "white-man" without thinking back 400 years and ahead
of Cruel and Unusual Punishment in this White Prison System.

But isn't that against the Eighth Amendment?
There's no justice for the 50 shades of brown
in this Criminal Injustice System.

I use to love the season of winter until I found out it's the white man's
favorite season;
The month of December or is it fall, November?

Either way, they rob melanin souls of their wages.
Let's not forget the taken of America, that dates back ages;
Natives and Blacks captured and harvested in cages.
Black names staining white paper, I'm talking of pages upon pages
at the New York Stock Exchange.

We celebrate Columbus Day, like he founded America.
Feast on thanksgiving without paying homage to the Native Indians.

And I'm not talking about the Cleveland Indians,
but they wear Red, White and Blue.
So, when I see the American Flag,
I see gallons of Our Red Blood Spilled by the White-men in Blue.

I will never attend Progressive Field.

Christopher Columbus, he was an Indian-Giver, an Indian-Killer.
Him and his white friends created smallpox, wrapped
them in blankets and
told them it would keep them warm during winter.
But then they died by the river.

I represent all 50 shades of brown,
from milk chocolate to Caramel
or is it Caramell?
Whatever it is, it's still brown.
My brothers and sisters with the lightest shades of color,
whose skin in the darkest of light is brighter than white
will never grow duller.

White isn't light anymore.
Brown is light and brown glow and as we grow,
let's not forget.

Let's not forget, that White ruined us.
White ruined us with dehumanization, degradation, miseducation,
stealing, injustice, and economic-castration.

And white people call us racists.

"White-boy," Black people don't have the power to be racists.
I repeat, "Blacks don't have the power to be racists."

Do you remember the castration?
Let me remind you of the Brutalization.

The butchering of our testes that prevented ejaculation
during the penetration
in the womb of our queens
that would have given birth to nations.

So, the next time you call us racist,
look up the definition and remember
what your white man have done to the African Nation.

"I DON'T DESERVE TO BE SHOT DOWN"

There's been an attack on the black man; I'm a black man still being attacked man, LISTEN!

I'm just a child. I'm just a black child. I'm just a black child with no identity; I was given a name by my parents that have no meaning.

"I don't deserve to be shot down"

I'm just a black child living in a community where leadership no longer exists. My dad abandoned me, ran to the streets, left me for dead, I don't know if he's dead or if he's in custody.

"I don't deserve to be shot down"

My mother left me home starving, chasing after another man whom she thought was a better man than my father. Child support spent upgrading her physical, to be intimate with his mental; he cheated on her, got another woman pregnant and said it was accidental.

"I don't deserve to be shot down"

He's back at home; he's doing her wrong, as if I'm invisible. He takes her money, beats her up and she's still in love with this criminal. She cooks him food, massages his mind, all I get is the $1 menu at McDonald's and Ramen Noodles all the time.

"I don't deserve to be shot down"

Never a hug, never a kiss, I get beaten with sticks and get slapped across the lips. I'm always sick, no remedies to do the trick, it's been two years since my last doctor visit.

"I don't' deserve to be shot down"
Time and money that should have been spent on me was wasted on irrelevant things, now I'm walking in this cold world with no shoes on my feet. Winter, no heat, Christmas, no tree, Santa Claus forgot all about me every Christmas morning.

"I don't deserve to be shot down"

Mama went to the club, she skipped the line, she sniffed the line, woke up the next morning in a hotel bed next to 3 guys who got inside her panty line. She didn't get paid, now she got AIDS, 3 years later she died from AIDS, no funeral arrangements had been made.

"I don't deserve to be shot down"

Even though there's light, I'm trapped in darkness, I'm lonely, I'm lost, where do I go? where do I start? No money, no food, I get picked on in school, the teachers don't care, they just smile and stare. Issues with school work, no time to solve it, but when fortunate kids raise their hands, they run in a hurry to solve it.

"I don't deserve to be shot down"

One step out the door, 100 feet to the corner, a mile around the block, there he is holding the glock. Lost in my community, what we are missing is unity, police supply the drugs, and drug dealers serve the community.

"I don't deserve to be shot down"

I called upon the creator to blossom this seed from the dark garden, with patience he shined the light upon me and I grew into a beautiful flower. I produced useful seeds, got rid of some useless weeds, please don't gun me down when I wear my hoodie to block the cool breeze.

"I don't deserve to be shot down"

4 years in a University, I got that degree, did a year for my masters, 2 more for my Ph.D. 100 grand in the hole, who's going to help me, went in for the interview, they didn't hire me.

"I don't deserve to be shot down"

I thought it was love, but it was lust, I gave her my all I thought I could trust. Her mom was gone, she was left with her dad all alone and all she felt was his thrust.

"I don't deserve to be shot down"

Her years of built anger released upon me, she wasn't prepared to love me, she skipped town, messed around, gave birth to two kids by two different men that made love to her and resembled her father.

My mama is gone; my heart is alone, where do I find the love?

WAKE UP

Wake Up, Wake Up;
they are enjoying the fruits of our labor and we are still starving.
Our schools look like shit,
they robbed us of our history and only teach us about
George Washington Carver.

We come from Kings and Queens, that's why we enjoy flashy things.
**But, that doesn't mean spend all your money on clothes,
Jordan's and flashy rings.**

Willie Lynch, he turned us against one another.
He got us saying, "yo daddy stupid, yo mama fat,
forget yo ugly sister and yo brother."

Here we are shooting each other dead,
they then rob us of our organs and sell them for millions
to those lying on their deathbed.

They arrange our death so they can live forever;
they plan shit like a terrible car accident that quickly sends us to heaven.
Young sisters are being picked up on their way home from school.
Young brothers hit in a drive-by near the neighborhood pool.

Racist white cops killing unarmed black teens.
Crime scene investigators reconstructing crime scenes.
CNN, Fox 8 and even the Plain Dealer,
lie to save the White Men, the Black Community Killers.

Wall Street is where they originally sold us,
something that the history books never told us.

We were the First Stock Sold.
In schools, our real history will never be told.

400 years of slavery, look how White America is living;
Big Banks, we extend our hand for a loan, $0 is given.

When we stepped off ship,
families were separated and thrown in cages.
Today, Black men are taken from their home and thrown in cages.

At the end of the sale, we were branded and paddled.
Thinking about joining a Greek organization?
Prepare to be branded and paddled.

Branded for ownership,
beaten for not using your new American name.
Some Greeks are insane. Yeah, they are out of their mind;
50 swats for not remembering your lines.

Education was a crime.
You could have been killed for learning.
**Now we got school, hate school, skip school,
and it affects our earnings.**

MILLENNIALS

Most of these Millennial parents turn their kid's school into a fashion
show;
they are more concerned about how their kids look,
than their kids being graduates though.

Mom said, "did you get the Jordan's yet? Or did you cop his polo?
The first day of school is tomorrow, he gotta be fresh for his photo."

Mom and dad face the mirror; all they got is their exterior.
Dropped out of high school, they're more comfortable dressing fly
and walking around with a hollow interior.

Every day is a fashion show, nothing else matter though.
They kill each other for attention, even their death is a fashion show.

Forget about the obituary; just make sure he's fresh up in the casket
though.

His obituary was empty; it was a waste of paper.
I only read about him chasing money and how he kept a fresh taper.

Meet Black On Black and his White friends; man, they are best friends.
They turn our homes into battlefields; they even kill lil black kids.

They boycotted Sorority Sisters, they forgot about Love and Hip Hop;
one of the main television shows that got our brains shot.

Milan and Brock, both wrestling cocks.
Mentally attacking our little brother's minds, acting like women,
man, this shit gotta stop.

Many Black women are torn in-between being Queens and niggas;
dressed as Goddesses, but with minds of Refugee killers.

"You were just another nigga on the hit list! Didn't they tell you that I
was a savage? Fuck your white horse and carriage!" The words of a Bad
Bitch."

Glorifying Beyoncé's, "Sorry," their words rain shots into their sons and
into men, like Cleveland did Timothy and Melissa. Murdering their
souls,
so they turn to the streets and foreign women for their required
attention.

Putting your fingers all in his face telling him boy bye,
now he's onto his next woman, while you're checking out her Instagram
settling for your late night drive-bys.

Y'all are sipping on that lemonade, Yonce still rich and married.
Her mission was to keep you broke and your love life buried.

I asked, **"What Would Happen if I Didn't Pray?"**
I was told that if I didn't, I wouldn't succeed.
That was a Lie.

I then asked, **"What Would Happen if I Didn't Believe?"**
I was told, if I didn't, I meant nothing and wouldn't be saved.
That was a Lie.

The truth was, if I wasn't grateful for all that was provided to me, both good and bad, and for the creator's creations, I wouldn't succeed. If I didn't believe in me, I wouldn't mean anything and wouldn't be able to save myself from the life I was provided earlier in life.

Now at age of 30, I have achieved everything that I have set forth to achieve without prayer and without violating the rights of another human being. I achieved my desires by expressing my gratitude daily for everything and everyone I encounter and by being respectful and treating others fairly. I inspire and add value to thousands of people daily as my way of giving back. I don't judge, I don't criticize, I don't have hatred, jealousy or envy in my spirit.

The church and baptism was forced upon me at a young age. At that time, I involuntarily accepted Jesus Christ as my personal savior. Now that I'm older, I have rejected the belief and have accepted the universal laws, my ancestors, parents, guardians, community leaders, and conscious educators as my personal saviors, because they helped paved my way out of captivity which helped me reach my full potential. Not the teachings of the church.

One of my biggest regrets was being baptized in a church at a very young age where I couldn't make the decision to reject it; in faucet water that gave me no connection to the universe, by a man who collaborates with oppressors by deceiving the people. That church didn't allow me to receive the greater universal connection I needed at the time. Instead, it prevented me from it.

THERE ARE THOSE WHO WILL ATTEMPT TO ASSASSINATE YOUR CHARACTER BECAUSE YOUR BELIEFS ARE OPPOSITE OF THEIRS.

In my opinion, these people are acknowledging the wrong power and have been miseducated. **There are only two powers, Good and Evil.** They are on the evil side. They have a satanic connection.

What work for some of us, don't work for all of us. If, so, everyone would look and live just alike.

Degrading a person's character based on what they choose to believe isn't righteous at all.

Dare to be different. **Dare to acknowledge and accept other people's differences.**

They teach us that we are poor, but **there are more white people on government assistance in America than there are African Americans.** They teach us that we can't afford a mortgage loan, but give lower interest rates to whites living in suburban communities. The projects were filled with whites once upon a time ago; until they got their low interest loan and left. That's when we moved in. Many whites still live there today.

They raise the interest rates on property for us because of segregation and skin color, not because we can't afford it. Those who didn't want to pay, who didn't want to be cheated, stayed in urban areas which we now refer to as the ghetto. The government then made our living situation worse.

Such information won't be advertised. The revolution won't be televised and they will never put our real history in school books.

STOP CRITICIZING MY PEOPLE FOR SHOWING THEIR BARE BODY WHEN WE MIGRATED FROM A VERY WARM CLIMATE WHERE CLOTHING WAS MINIMUM.

Clothes are gatekeepers for bacteria and diseases.

All parts of our body need exposure to sunlight. Sunlight feeds us, gives us energy and helps fight off infections.

Living in warm climates was our natural way of life, until we were kidnapped by Europeans from the motherland and brought to a foreign land and climate.

So when you see our bare skin in the summer, embrace it!

People have the right to dress however they wish, they don't need a signed permission slip from you or anyone else, as to when and where they can undress themselves. You aren't caring for those people.

As far as honoring or dishonoring parents, many parents aren't even knowledgeable about the importance of sunlight or how energy works. If they are discouraged by their child's body, it's because they have been influenced by the negative influences of others, those who live life criticizing others like hypocrites of spiritual institutions.

Part of self-expression and owning who you are is doing what you believe is true for you to do. Not the opinions of the world, not a religion, not the government, but what is true for you to do. **If a sister chooses to pop out her breasts to feed her baby while in a public place, it is her right to do so. It's her body and her baby need to be fed.** If she wishes to wear less clothing during the summer, it's her right to. You or anyone else isn't providing her clothing or providing anything else for her but an opinion with no value of how she should be.

If you are ashamed of our people's bare bodies, close your eyes and stayed hidden in your four walls. Our bodies are made to be revealed.

Don't beat yourself up for getting a poor grade in English.
It's not our original language. The use of Emoji is how we once
communicated.

They brought it back and installed them in our smartphones.
We can thank them for that.

But now they are upset because we use them to communicate and many
people are unable to understand what we are implying.

**Many people try to bash our language of Slang because we created
a better way for us to communicate,** instead of properly using the
English Language.

Be proud that we are still able to create our own form of
communication.

Don't kill yourself over the misuse of the English Language.
It's ok, if you mess it up, other foreigners do it all the time and they get by.

BLACK HISTORY

Black History isn't just about the past, or the past contributions of those who came before us who have made popular headlines.

Black History is not just about being the first black man or woman to accomplish something.

Black History is not just about how many followers and honors one has received in their lifetime.

Black History isn't just about the month of February.

Black History is you and me, our culture and our existence.

Black History is present twenty-four hours a day and seven days a week. You breathing is Black History in itself.

The world wouldn't have what it has now if it wasn't for the creation of the first human being, who was a black woman. Her name was not Eve.

So, don't limit the celebration of our race and culture to 28 days a year. Celebrate it 365 days a year.

The world wouldn't revolve if it wasn't for the black men, women and children walking the earth today, as well as those who have left us.

Asia wouldn't be Asia, Europe wouldn't be Europe and America wouldn't be America.

Oh, and John Glenn would have never gone Outer Space and Neil Armstrong would have never touched foot on the moon if it wasn't for our black people.

WE ARE MORE THAN JUST A COLOR

We are the stars, the earth, the sun and the moon,
We are perfectly aligned with pyramids, creating birthday signs and seasons,
like Cancers kicking off the summer in June.

We Are More Than Just A Color

We are Pangaea; we are Africa, the birthplace of civilization,
We roamed the world first; our founding mother gave birth to this nation.

We Are More Than Just A Color

We are the diamonds and gold, your oils and fruits,
We are the coco to your chocolate bar,
and rubber to your boots

We Are More Than Just A Color

We are the spirits and vibrations, the language and rules,
The numbers, religion, science, inventions and tools.

We Are More Than Just A Color

We are the plants and medicines, the philosophies and health,
the combs, the brushes, the beauty, and the wealth.

We Are More Than Just A Color

We are the hunters and fishermen, the blueprints and machines,
we are the homes and their keys, the jackets and jeans.

We are electricity, we are the phones,
we are the cars in the street, we are the firewood
and coal that provide the buildings we've built with heat.

We Are More Than Just A Color

We are the music, the films, the arts and sports,
mother liberty is really an African woman,
you know the statue in New York?

The French gave it to America as a gift
because they wanted our enslavement to end,
America changed her features, kept us in plantations
feeding cotton to gin.

We Are More Than Just A Color

We are the stocks and bonds, we are Wall Street,
We are the victories of War,
with no honorable mentions on history sheets.

In 1921, our rich town was burned to concrete,
because after we won WWI,
many white Americans had no money or no place to sleep.
As a result, they turned into wolves and we turned into sheep.

We Are More Than Just A Color

We are not Negros, Pickaninnies,
monkeys, nor apes, we are the original royal family,
that society took centuries to reshape.

We Are More Than Just A Color

Most of the world doesn't want you to know
how great you really are,
that's why they hide it away, feed us illusions
and have torn our families apart.

We Are More Than Just People On The Back Of The Bus,

almost everything you see and do,
you can believe it originated from us.

We Are More Than Just A Color

We are 365 days a year,
We are the most intelligent beings alive,
Let's celebrate that with cheer.

So many of us dedicate so much time and effort ensuring our people, especially our children are given the necessary tools needed to progress in life, but we have people who create great platforms for our people and recognize people on their platform who deliberately live their lives tearing our community and children apart, which defeats the purpose of what we are doing.

How can you consider yourself a great parent, leader or role model, man and or woman, when you allow people to poison the minds of your little ones and you glorify them? You praise and award them?

You are deliberately collaborating with our oppressors plans of destroying our culture by shining light on those who are encouraging your daughter to grow up to be a sex slave for material possessions that have no value and who are encouraging your son to grow up and violate the rights of other men and their families, just so they can shine with someone else's prized possessions. Those who aren't teaching them the IMPORTANCE of hard work, leadership, perseverance and how to respect and treat our most important creations on earth, Our African Women.

I will not wish such people success on their platforms or future endeavors unless, they recognize their behaviors, apologize to the community at large for such behaviors, and revamp their organization, shining light on those who are truly uplifting and inspiring our people.

I highly suggest you read, Chapter 4: I Am My Brothers and Sisters Keeper in "Cultivating Minds To Own Thyself."

Many of us make anywhere between $20,000 – $60,000 annually and won't have that saved at retirement. #OverTimeWontHelp

The fancy stuff is all good now **until we punch our last clock and notice we've worked our whole life for a 1/2 of a million or more and have nothing to show for it.**

$20,000 a year for 30 years of work = $600,000

$60,000 a year for 30 years of work = $1,800,000

AVOID THE RAT RACE AND RETIRE YOUNG AND WEALTHY.

Here is some financial literacy advice for you:

SAVING YOUR ALL YOUR MONEY IN YOUR BANK'S SAVINGS ACCOUNT REALLY GIVES YOUR MONEY NO VALUE.

Let me show you how:

-- The Rule of 72 -- a simplified way to determine how long an investment will take to double, given a fixed annual rate of interest. By dividing 72 by the annual rate of return, investors can get a rough estimate of how many years it will take for the initial investment to duplicate itself.

Formula: "Years to double = 72 / Interest Rate"

- Let's say you invest $100.00 into your savings account at 3% interest; it will take 24 years before you see $200.00.

- Let's say you invest that $100.00 into an investment account at 6% interest; it will take 12 years before you see $200.00

Most saving accounts have less than 3% interest.

Here's what happens when you invest into a 9% or 12% account:

• At 9%, it will take 8 years to see your $200
• At 12%, it will take 6 years to see your $200

JUST IMAGINE IF YOU INVESTED MORE MONEY INTO 9% and 12% Accounts.

IT'S IMPOSSIBLE TO SUPPORT EVERYBODY.

If you try, you will find yourself defeated, financially, physically, spiritually, mentally and emotionally. You will find yourself disconnected from those who need you most (your loved ones) because you'd be taking time and resources from them

Don't allow others to bring you down, take you from you, because they criticize you for not supporting them. Focus on being a crutch for those whom you wish to help.

For those of you who are support seekers, those in your following may not be into what you are promoting and that's okay. You can't force someone to like you or your product. Also, refrain from speaking poorly about them. Focus your energy on your target audience and work on your pitch. **Don't get discouraged because people tell you "no." Keep working toward your goal.**

I contacted thousands of individuals and organizations to sponsor the release of How Success Became My Focus and Cultivating Minds To Own Thyself. I received 0 Calls, 0 Text messages and 0 Emails. My books are available at all major book retailers because of my own personal investment.

Support seekers, your biggest supporters may be those whom you have never met, who is waiting to see, and/or hear your pitch. The better you are at communicating, and the more people you communicate with within your target audience, the better your chances are in succeeding in your industry.

Nothing is handed, EVERYTHING IS EARNED!

It's unfair to your family
to donate to someone else's
funeral fund, **who have
spent their whole life**
purchasing everything
except life insurance.

I ROSE

As she opened her mouth,
her tongue cocked back like the hammer
on Darren Wilson's 4-5, releasing hollow tips into my soul
and into my mind, impairing my spine.

Rupturing the vertebral column she once supported.

So Then I Rose...

I rose to my feet wondering,
how could the one I gave my all to,
turn her back on me and attack me so viciously?

She once stood behind me to catch my fall,
right beside me to conquer it all.
She was the one I held closely in bed, who kept me ahead.

Her once rich spirit has been consumed by Beyoncé's "Sorry".
911, what's your emergency? Yes, he hit me.
I lied, Nigga you gotta go, I ain't sorry.

She called the ones, who lynch black men
for being black men to lynch an innocent black man.

All over a late night text from a friend, and
a pair of Red Bottoms I couldn't afford for her birthday.

Stripped of my freedom and of all my possessions,
I still dreamed of a rightful Queen as my blessing.

3 months later, released from the county jail,
not a letter sent through the county mail,
she awaits at the door. "Baby I'm sorry," I've missed you,
I'm never going to let this happen to you again. I promise.

So Then I Rose...

I rose wondering, who was this
mysterious woman apologizing and making promises to
never harm me again?

Who are you? I said.
She responds, I'm your Queen.
My Queen? Yes, your Queen.
I've heard your dreams.

What she has done to you was wrong,
I'm here to serve on your throne.
My King.

09

BREAKFAST IN HEAD

How can you expect anyone to accept you, when you don't accept yourself?

How can you expect anyone to love you, when you don't love yourself?

You must put you before any other spiritual being that's living a human experience just like you.

Hit the Like Button for Everything You Produce.

Society has made you believe that you must take care of everyone else first and then take care of you after you have done so. The truth is this; you will never get to you, if you continue to think that way. You are important and society doesn't want you to believe that you are.

You find it difficult to accept you, to love you and to invest in your dreams because you have been programmed to operate in the best interest of others and not yourself.

It's time that you claim that number one spot.

The things you've survived made you who you are today.
Despite your mother's mistakes and your father's mistakes,
**the creator still held onto you and brought you to smile again,
to love again and to have joy.**

**You have been blessed with life again,
there's nothing more valuable than life itself.**

Eliminate Fear and Worry.
You have been given another opportunity. Set Yourself Free!

Those who have threatened to harm you and who have harmed
you emotionally, mentally, spiritually, and physically, have already
harmed themselves.

No need to seek revenge, the damage is already done.

This is your chance to fly again.

SET YOURSELF FREE
BY LOVING YOURSELF FIRST

Every morning, enter your bathroom or
somewhere in your home where there's
a mirror, if you have a body mirror, that
would be perfect.

Before applying makeup/foundation,
grooming your hair, brushing your teeth
and putting on clothes, look in the mirror
for a minute or two and repeat, "I love you
for whom you are and I refuse to be controlled
by what others think, say and do." Then smile.

The purpose of this exercise is to get you
to love yourself and to free yourself.

Many people spend time trying to fit in with
society or trying to live up to someone else's
standards instead of their own. Loving you
**and refusing to be deployed by the thoughts and
actions of others helps you become self-disciplined,
and it helps you to live out your purpose.**

When given the chance to identify you, give
your own definition of you. Let others know
how you perceive yourself and show them that
you have ownership of your life. If not, they will
decide to and will control your life for you.

BEING JUST BEAUTIFUL IS NOT ENOUGH.

Be Fruitful, Exciting, Fun, Inspiring, Crazy,
Aggressive and Selfless.

Be who you set out to be, not
what the world has decided for you to be.

Be your own amazing self.
You are more than Beautiful.

TODAY, YOU HAVE
ANOTHER OPPORTUNITY

Today is an opportunity to change
things you have the ability to change
and to start afresh from yesterday's mistakes.

Today is an opportunity to love again,
promote love, build one another up
and to make new friends.

Drake had you saying, "No New Friends,"
but how many of your current friends are
encouraging you to live a better life?

How many are encouraging you to drink,
smoke, abuse drugs and to throw your life
away without actually saying it?

Make friends that are uplifting and inspiring.

Use this opportunity to create a plan to help
provide a better environment for you and
your family.

**"Remember to smile, because you are alive
and every breath taken is another opportunity
to become a better you."**

You Can't Expect Someone To Support You When You've Given Up On You.

When you invest in you, supporters may invest in you.
But only when you've proven yourself to be disciplined,
dedicated and persistent.

Why should anyone invest more effort in you than you?

No one wants to waste their time and resources on someone
who isn't sure about the direction they are headed in.

**You have to continue to work on you and stop crying about
people not supporting you.**

Nobody owes you anything, but you owe you everything.

*I invest in all areas of me so that I'm able to achieve whatever it is
I desire in life, whether it be with the help of others or the carrying of my
own weight.*

DON'T DEPEND ON LUCK

Luck doesn't come around often
and when it comes, it's least
expected.

With faith, effort, hard-work,
dedication, determination, and
persistence, you can kind of predict
your outcome.

You will sustain bed sores waiting
around for Luck. You will spend
hundreds of thousands of dollars
waiting on Luck.

Waiting around for Luck will have
you growing old, **wishing you had
invested in you sooner.**

My Great, Great, Great, Great, Great-Grandfather
was tortured and killed waiting on Jesus.

Don't let that be you.

Frederick Douglass said,
**"I prayed for twenty years
but received no answer until I
prayed with my legs."**

WHAT IS YOUR WHY?

We all have a story to share.
We all have experienced some
things in life that could have prevented
us from moving forward.

But what kept us going was
our "WHY."

When we figured out our why,
we pushed through the very obstacles
that they said were too difficult.

**It's only difficult if you haven't
utilized the steps placed before you.**

So, after discovering your why,
take one step, one leap, one jog,
one sprint, and one mile at a time.

If you remain still, you won't have
the chance to move forward.

TAKE THE NEXT STEP

If you don't take risks,
how will you grow?

In fact, how will you
secure your desires?

You can't succeed if you are
trapped in your comfort zone.

Take the next step.

Don't ask someone to do it with you,
to do it for you, or to go with you,
JUST TAKE THE NEXT STEP.

It's your life and your desires
that is on the line.

Don't cry over the past, it's gone.
Don't stress about the future, it hasn't arrived.
Live in the present and make the most of it.

Glorify your imperfections and just work on
progress in all areas of your life.

**Accept your mistakes, failures, hurt, pain and
the uncomfortable experiences,** for they will help
mold you into the person you are destined to become.

Also take risks, don't stay trapped in your comfort zone.

You will do just fine if you believe in you and have faith.

Fear, Worry and Faith do not occupy the same space.

You Have to Witness the Storm before Sunshine.

Even with Sunshine,
it has to rain in order for trees to grow.

THE LIGHT AFTER THE STORM

After fighting through storm after storm,
without giving up, life became easier for me.

Those experiences have prepared me to
hurdle obstacles that may arise, with poise
and gratitude.

When you give up on you, **everything
around you eventually gives up and falls
down on you.**

But when you invest in you, pushing
through to the next level with no intention
of giving up, the wall eventually gives in
and breaks. Setting you free.

There's No Rock Bottom

Even when you think
you are at Rock Bottom,
you aren't even at Rock
Bottom, because you haven't
been suppressed beneath the
tectonic plates beneath the
surface of the Earth.

**So, get up and go get what
you deserve.**

Faith overrides everything.

If you ask and believe,
then you shall receive.

YOUR CAREER CHOICE SHOULD NOT ONLY ELEVATE YOUR POCKETS BUT YOUR INTELLIGENCE.

If you are living just to make money, you are missing out on so much more. Especially on you.

Learning should never become an ending process for you.
Always be willing to learn whenever you can, from whomever you can because one day you will be glad that you did.

I Don't Struggle With Bills because I am grateful for what I have and I live within my means.

- I am happy that I have running water, so, I'm grateful when the water bill comes.

- I am happy to have lights, so, I'm grateful when the light bill comes.

- I am happy to have heat, so, I'm grateful when the gas bill comes.

- I am happy to have insurance on my items, so, I'm grateful when the insurance bill comes.

- I am happy to have life insurance, so I'm grateful when the life insurance bill comes.

As happy as you get when you purchase something you really want, **you should be just as happy when you pay for something you need.** Instead of complaining about bills, be grateful for them.

No one is responsible for the debt you've acquired on your own.

If you are trying to be with someone because you are financially illiterate and you want that person to bail you out, **you deserve to be by yourself.**

You are a liability; you are a bad credit.

Stop walking around with your hand out as if people who've worked hard for theirs owe you something, because they don't.

You owe yourself everything.

Pay Yourself Before Paying A Bill.

I often ask people what is the first thing they do with their money once they get paid. The most common response is,
"I Pay My Bills."

Many of us put everyone before ourselves which isn't the best thing to do. We are taxed when we earn, meaning taxes are withdrawn from our checks for our hard labor and we are taxed when we spend our money including on the bills we pay.

You should work on paying you first which gives the power to you and not the bill collectors. Every earning you receive take a portion of it and pay you first (Save/Invest), then pay your bills, purchase your necessities and buy what you want after.

In the case you aren't able to cover your expenses such as bills, just put what you can on them or find other ways to generate money without touching the money you paid you with. That way you aren't flat broke before the next pay period and you will still be in control, not your bill collectors. **Overcome your fear of bill collectors by being in control of your money.**

If you are having a hard time paying cable, internet and phone etc., cut them until you can afford them without hassle. Invest that extra money into you.

Don't worry about the harassing phone calls from bill collectors, because they will only call. Tell them you only have it in cash and that they can come pick it up, lol

You require others to be Upfront with you,
but when You look in the Mirror,
You are Nowhere to Be Found.

You cannot expect someone to give you their all when you haven't
given your all to you. When you don't know who you are.

You have to be honest with the real you first, before expecting someone
to give you 100% of them.

You cry about someone switching up on you, when you have never revealed
the true you to them.

The next time you look in the mirror, show the real you and not your
costume. Then show the real you to those who you require to be upfront
with you. Then build from there.

STUPID

Stop Declaring People Stupid;
People don't have to live according
to your standards or perceptions.

If your way of living was the correct
and only way to live, everyone would
be built and developed exactly just as
you are. But they are not.

So because they are not, **they are entitled
to live anyway they desire.** Even the guy
with his top down on Interstate 480 West
in Cleveland during winter blizzards.

You may have fertilized her ovum, or you
may have pushed them out, but neither of
you created life.

So, focus on getting rid of your negative
tendencies and embrace those who
chose to live uncommonly.

It's not an issue to want others
to see the good in us.

**But it is an issue if we allow
others to determine our value.**

They may be able to pick
the petals off your stem,
but they can never **destroy
your roots.**

RIDING YOUR TRAIN

There are individuals who will
hop on your train and ride it to
your destination.

There are those, who will not get
on at all.

There are those who will walk in
front of it and who may get ran
over.

Then, there are those who will hop
on and get right off.

When those individuals hop off, **keep
the engine started and keep heading
toward your desired destination.**

Don't delay your arrival to your destination,
for individuals who have given up on you.

Once you arrive, there will be a whole new
town of people welcoming you, who will be
excited to aboard your cabin.

Practice Tuning Out those Distractions that Keep You from Being the Best You!

Growing up, many adults had issues with youth wearing earphones/headphones,

"It's not safe… they can't hear what's going on… blah blah blah."

If you are anything like me, I don't wear my earphones /headphones just to listen to music and to feel the vibrations rattle my eardrums.

I apply my electronic devices to tune out negative thoughts, people, music and vibes that play on the subconscious mind in attempt to destroy me from who I am.

One of my strongest abilities is my ability to ignore.

With that, it has allowed me to define, identify and to accept thyself, as well as to achieve everything that I have set out to achieve.

So, wear your headphones or earphones to block out unwelcome energy, so that you can tune in to creating a life worth living for.

Don't lose yourself in the process of helping
others achieve their desires;

ALWAYS make time for you,
doing what you desire.

You bust your ass making sure they won't drown
writing their story.

Will they do the same for you?

Write your own story because they won't!

If you have a lot going on for yourself
and there are people depending on you,

**hanging with someone who have nothing
to lose may eventually cause you to lose
everything you have.**

Your Freedom; Your Life.

As soon as you begin to feel
Someone **WEIGHING DOWN** your
potential, **ESCAPE!!!**

Spread your wings and fly.
Don't allow sandbags to keep
you from soaring.

CONTRAST

You do not have to explain
yourself to anyone about
how different you are.

If they can't sense it
with their own set of eyes
and vibes, **let them be blind.**

If they are blinding you
with your past, **step to
the side** and allow
someone else to help
you see ahead.

There are those who are
holding onto your past.

Kindly tell them to let go
because you are no longer
captive.

You are free.

Do not accept an apology based on the fancy words that are delivered to you,
which could possibly be the words of someone else, but accept the apology based upon their actions taken. That's how you know if their apology is sincere or not.

Taking accountability for our actions is more than just words, but the steps we take forward in preventing us from making the same poor decisions we've made again. This can take longer than a few seconds, minutes, hours, a day, month or even a year.

So, don't be so quick to forgive others when no real effort has been put forth, and be willing to hold yourself accountable for the poor decisions you make. We have to challenge others to do better, as well as ourselves, so that we can earn our dignity and succeed on our journey of life.

Do not allow others to smile in front of your red dot,
who didn't appreciate you before it came on.

That is your moment. **Shine.**

LOVE ISN'T SELFISH.
LOVE IS AN ABUNDANCE.

DON'T ALLOW OTHERS TO BE SELFISH WITH YOUR LOVE.

Spread it across the world. **People are in need of it.**

A selfish person shouldn't be able to hold your love hostage for them.

My time isn't for you to have all to yourself.
The moment I feel you become selfish with it,
**will be the moment my time with you begin to
expire!**

Just like we have the power
to attract our own successes,
we have the power to attract
those who are good for us.

Who you attract is a result of
the energy you choose to emit.

You can't help those who
do not wish to be helped.
You can't teach those who
do not wish to learn.

Do not waste valuable time
and energy. **Invest it on
those who can benefit from
you.**

Just because the Sun isn't out
doesn't mean you can't Shine.

Come Out of Your Cloud and
Light Up the Place.

CLEANSE YOUR MIND

Let's kick off the moment by Shaking
Off yesterday's baggage and worries.

Here is a fresh opportunity to feed your
mind with positive fruits and vegetables.

**Cleanse your mind of negative thoughts by
feeding it with positive images, music, books and
people.**

Negative thoughts affect your body's systems,
creating disease and disaster.

After cleansing your mind, cleanse your body and
environment. Your vision will then clear and with it comes
a feeling of relief.

Sooner or later, there will be the manifestation
of good. Be in health, happiness or supply.

Burned Bridges can be rebuilt;
put aside your ego, take self-accountability,
ask for forgiveness and get to work.

Often times we tend to give credit to other sources for our achievements without thanking ourselves.

You carried it out. **Give Yourself Credit.**

10
MAGNANIMITY

If people can't see pass their own emotions, problems, dreams and personal successes, their relationship with others will eventually become rocky and fall apart.

You must stand on the edge of the cliff and see the entire horizon. Not onshore, viewing from the same level as those who are afraid to rise.

FRIENDSHIPS

Friendships shouldn't be sprints, but 3Ks and Marathons:

I admire Cross-Country and Marathon Runners because we
know instant gratification and short sprints won't amount to much.

I'm a long distance runner, not an individual who gives up easily or
who looks to acquire something quickly and easily.

Friends equipped with Patience, Leadership and Strength to climb to
the top of the hill, pushing through to cruise down the other-side together
without arguing, fighting and sabotaging each other's character, are the
friends worth having.

BE OF SERVICE TO OTHERS

I'd like to share a testimony. Not for recognition or rewards, but for you to see what kind of heart I have and to see how tithes can be paid outside of a spiritual institution.

As I walked into the Waffle House one early morning with a cousin of mine and her friend in Columbus, Georgia, an older Caucasian guy, whom from my eyes appeared to be in need of food was sitting on the curb outside the Waffle House. As my cousin and her friend proceeded into the restaurant, I approached the gentleman and asked, "Are You Hungry? Do You Want Some Food?" And he replied, "sure." **I ordered him his food of choice and blessed him with an early breakfast.**

The creator places people and situations before us to see how we will react to them. The spirit of the creator operates within those in need as well as those who aren't. How we treat its creations is how it chooses to treat us.

Though I'm far from religious, I pay my tithes by being of service to others. You must know that tithes don't just have to be paid in a collection plate at a spiritual institution; you may do so by being of service to others.

Make it your duty to add value (not just monetary value) to those you come in contact with continuously and unconditionally.

We know there are rotten fruits and potatoes in baskets we can't save. We know that if you plant a seed for a tree to grow, that tree isn't going to grow overnight. We know that all students don't learn the same way, because if they did, everyone would have graduated with honors.

I have this to say, pick over those who can't be saved and If you are able, **have patience and invest in those who can, and those who are willing to grow.**

IT'S NOT ALWAYS ABOUT YOU, WHAT ABOUT US?

So many are focused on individual achievements; a college degree, home, car, money, clothes, jewelry, etc.

But What About "We" Achievements?

Don't get me wrong, individual achievements are amazing. You are supposed to do those things. You are supposed to be intelligent, have a shelter over your head, have clothes on your back, have a form of transportation, have a source of income, know how to feed yourself and so forth...

What team goals have you set?
What team related achievements can you speak of?
What are you doing for others to help get them to the next level?
How are you getting your team to the next level?

Most relationships, teams and organizations fail because one or more members operate with the "I, Me, My, and Mine" mentality, instead of the "We" mentality.

When joining a team, whether it's a relationship, a sport, a business, an organization etc., take "I, Me, My and Mine" out of the equation and focus on the We.

You + Me = We

We can achieve greater things than I could achieve without You and you without **Me.**

A GREAT LIFE IS A BALANCED LIFE

Don't kill yourself working 2-3 jobs
or crazy hours of overtime.

Your family need you.

Money is important, **but not important
Enough to risk your life, and your family
over it.**

Develop enough skil and intelligence to
secure a position tha will take the place of
those two jobs and those crazy hours of
overtime so you can have time for those whom matter
most and enjoy the life you desire.

It's unfair to your family,
to be called in on your off
day and **you not ask for a bonus.**
They matter too.

As we prepare for each Holiday Season, lets also prepare to be generous and empathic towards those who may be experiencing Depression. Depression and thoughts of Suicide are high around this time of year.

Many of our women will become more emotional and vulnerable due to the absence of a loved one or the absence of a good male mate in the home. Many will start to break down when they see full families come together for gatherings. Many will turn to social media and television, and instantly develop a sense of jealousy when they see happy couples. Some may become more upset and turn to drugs and alcohol to numb the pain, which could possibly lead to suicide because they aren't able to find someone to love them and their family the way other women and their family are being loved.

Our women may become emotionally needy, which isn't good because their emotions may take the place of their intelligence, allowing a man who's not good for them to enter her home and body, putting her health, safety and family at risk, just to fill a temporary void. Also, they may begin beating themselves up for not being able to provide for their children on the holidays, as they are already struggling to provide their necessities. Some may risk their freedom by attempting to shoplift from retailers.

Many of our men will experience depression as well. Especially those whom are incarcerated. Many will experience a loss of hope, reality, and sense of importance. Many will become hurt inside because they can't provide for their family or be with their family. Some may not have any at all. Some will consider suicide.

Those who aren't incarcerated but don't have a source of income, may become hurt inside because they can't provide for their family either.

Their emotions may take the place of their intelligence and they may violate the rights of another human-being just to provide for themselves and their family. Such actions may cause harm or death to either them or their victims, or they may become incarcerated, and all families involved will experience grief during the time love is supposed to be present.

As I mentioned earlier, Depression and thoughts of Suicide is high around the holiday season and what I mentioned above aren't the sole causes of depression and suicide, there's a ton of factors. The point is, it's important that you make yourself available to those who will need emotional support; Love.

If you know someone whose behavior starts to change; those who begin engaging in risky behaviors, becoming upset, angry, distancing themselves from others, are experiencing a loss of appetite, giving away personal items, stating they no longer want to be here anymore, etc., don't leave them. Stay and help them through it. If you aren't able to help, contact someone who can and **contact the National Suicide Prevention Lifeline at 1-800-273-8255 if they have thoughts of suicide.**

Allow your spirit of love to flow free as the leaves in autumn and the creations of the universe will support you.

REMARKS FROM THE AUTHOR

Hi, you have finally made it to the other end, thank you for supporting In Between These Sheets. What are your thoughts? Quite interesting content don't you think?

I welcome your review of this book on one or more of the major book platforms.

Before I let you go, I would like to share with you my final remarks:

As people from unfortunate backgrounds looking to achieve something greater for ourselves, our loved ones and for our community, we have to get rid of the mindset that everyone owes us something because we had a troubled past, have a troubled present and a hopeless future. We all can write books and books on all we have endured, but our struggles shouldn't be used as a crutch to gain success. Struggles are part of the process of becoming great. No great person has had a clear problem free path to their greatness. No one owes us anything, but we owe ourselves everything. Hard work beats talent and a panhandler may never receive much. Frederick Douglass once said, **"I Prayed for Twenty Years but Received No Answer until I Prayed with My Legs."**

One of the keys to becoming great is giving your all to you, unveiling new layers of you, and helping you become better. Walk in purpose, walk in dignity, walk with love and love every part of you. **PASSION + EFFORT = RESULTS.**

Please note, greatness isn't just about what you have achieved for yourself, but those whom you have inspired and have helped become better. So, allow your pot to boil over to unthaw the iceberg that's keeping people trapped from becoming their greater self. **Mission is greater than self.**

I was chosen by the creator of all beings to develop knowledge of self, take control of self, to get rid of negative tendencies from my subconscious mind, to be magnanimous, and to become a mature, successful, educated and responsible adult.

I have given you the tools,
but I can't do your work for you.
**If I do your work,
then my work will be left undone.**

I now challenge you to go on and make your mark somewhere in this universe. Don't forget to take this book with you.
On Your Mark! Get Set! Goooo!

CONTRIBUTORS

EXECUTIVE ASSISTANT

Cleveland Native, Jessica Danelle Bacon is an amazing mother, friend, Professional Hair Braider, and an Event Coordinator and Executive Assistant to internationally known Author and Speaker Jameel Davis; together indubitably assisting both younger and older men and women in discovering their purpose. Since 2016, Jessica has been a protégé of Davis, who has helped and who continues to help her in the areas of personal and professional development. Jessica is a highly impressionable and persistent woman who connects naturally with individuals in ways they will never forget. She enjoys creating and elevating platforms for aspiring creative professionals; encouraging them to break out of their shell and to share their many gifts and talents.

Jessica known in the artistic community as Nina Lem is a floetic artist who writes poetic and musical pieces created through feeling. She has performed her poetry and music at The Cleveland Job Corps Center, Daniel E. Morgan K-8 School, The Kultivation Theater and at many local open mic venues.

"Poetry, rap, and singing allow me to be free from rules or boundaries.

It's my own masterpiece that I express to the world, proudly representing my roots, melanin, and the values, morals, and principals we all need in this generation."
- I am Nina Lem (melanin) aka Jessica Bacon.

Jessica's free flowing spirit has allowed her to share wonderful moments with celebrities Charlie Wilson, Teyana Taylor, Iman Shumpert, Lil Duval, Mo'nique, Tommy Davidson and many more. She has appeared on 93.1 WZAK Relationship Hour with radio personality Sam Sylk. In October 2018, Jessica was selected to feature on the hit television show, Divorce Court which aired on January 24, 2019. Jessica Bacon a true humanitarian, a lover of people devoted to helping people from different walks of life, loves meeting new people, traveling and having fun.

Connect with Jessica on Social Media:

FB: Jessica D. Bacon
Instagram: @Connect_with_Jess

EDITOR

Idierukevebe Raphael is a Writer and Editor with great creativity skills that cut across most top niche in the writing industry. His proficiency in writing is clearly seen in the series of great content and articles that he has written over the past 5 years. He is well known for his precision in editing several online articles and contents, proofreading numerous books, articles, blog posts and Website contents for different clients in different parts of the world

His eyes for details and passion for creating top notch quality and flawless content has been the leading force driving him in the writing industry.

You can connect with Raphael on:
FB: Idierukevbe Raphael
Email: raphael.idierukevbe@gmail.com

CREATIVE DIRECTOR

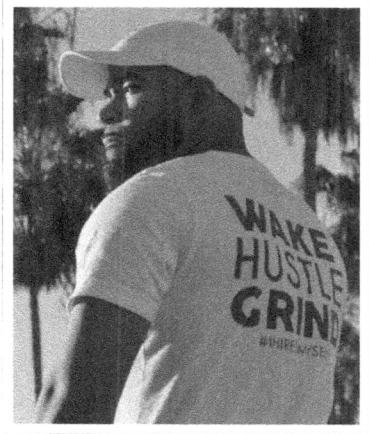

Kevin Conwell Jr. is a self-made serial entrepreneur; #Ihiredmyself, Wakehustlegrind.com , self-published author, founder of 3KP Marketing & ClevelandMediaCompany. com , Expert Graphic Designer, Creative Director, Fashion Designer, and Social Media Expert!

Kevin earned his degree from Cleveland State University in Marketing and Business Communications. Kevin is a catalyst for those who are in leadership and management roles who need assistance in bringing their entrepreneurial ideas to life. Kevin converts their ideas, breathing magic into them by making them into online websites, print media, t-shirts and graphics. Kevin also has helped other fashion brands come up with design concepts as well as media campaigns. Kevin is no stranger to hard work and he will execute any project with passion and dedication.

Connect with Kevin on Instagram @WakeHustleGrind_Ceo

CREATIVE WRITING COACH

Tonisha "NeeNeeMarie" Glover, M.Ed. is a Cleveland native who grew up modestly in the inner city. She was raised by a single mother of three and comes from a large extended family of cousins, aunties and uncles that refers to her as Nee Nee, a childhood nickname that followed her into adulthood. She carries with her a host of memories from her early years; some pleasant and some difficult to digest, such as the domestic violence she witnessed growing up. "Life ain't been no crystal stair" (Hughes, 1994), but Tonisha was determined to make a better life for herself.

Tonisha has always had a natural passion and appreciation for creativity and the arts. She expressed herself mostly through poetry, dance and theater as a teenager. These premature talents resulted in an offer for a full tuition scholarship to Ohio University for theater. She contemplated the idea for weeks before eventually refusing the offer. Although she absolutely loved the arts she decided to attend Kent State University. She received a Bachelor's degree in education and a Master's degree in Higher Education and Student Personnel. Tonisha believed that education was a way out of poverty and a distinct path for success and opportunities that she would have been denied otherwise.

After receiving her graduate degree, Tonisha decided to return to the Cleveland area with her toddler son to give back and serve her community through higher education. There, she serves as a coordinator and college advisor for high school students taking college courses. She found that she enjoys working with youth from the inner city and preparing them for post-secondary education. Now that her educational appetite is mostly satisfied, Tonisha has had a returning hunger for creativity with words. She has begun to write and express herself freely through poetry and short stories once more, only this time, from the perspective of a mother, spiritual being, Black woman, mental health advocate and pescatarian with more life experiences than before.

Tonisha hopes to finish and publish her first project within the next 1-2 years. She is determined and passionate about sharing authentic, yet entertaining stories that people across the world can relate to and/or learn from.

She invites you to follow her path via social media **Instagram: @ itsneeneemarie. Stay tuned.**

WARDROBE DESIGNER & FASHION STYLIST

Cierra Hicks is a self-taught fashion designer. Her elegant and contemporary fashions are custom designed.

Her collections exemplify modern class and style that will increase your self-assurance during your casual evening.

Each gourmet is designed with precision that accents your body's assets for all occasions. Cierra's designs will make you feel complete.

Connect with Cierra on Instagram @Ci_Sews

PHOTOGRAPHER

Demarcus Lett aka Jedi Arts is a self-taught Photographer, Videographer, Front-end Developer, and is passionately curious. He tends to play way too much video games and loves to workout. He believes knowledge is power which is why he always tries to learn something new. His dream is to impact as many people as he can in his lifetime, through design, charity or just a simple hello.

To learn more about Jedi Arts please check out his work at www.JediaArtsproductions.com and be ready to be amazed.

PHOTOGRAPHER / VIDEOGRAPHER

Starting from humble beginnings in the blooming art district of Canton, Ohio, Overlord began with a simple goal: to change the mixed-media landscape. To create waves in not only music, film, or fashion, but art as a whole. Together, we hope to create something genuine and new, something that will change a generation.

– Quinton Ailes aka Q. Presents, Founder.

OVERLORDCOLLECTIVE
MUSIC · FILM · CLOTHING

Connect with Q via email at Q.Presents@gmail.com and on Instagram @Qpresents

MASTER BARBER

Sunshyne Cannon born and raised in the suburbs of Cleveland is a very creative and goal-driven barber.

She began her career at Labarberia Institute of Hair in 2014. After receiving her Master Barber License from Labarberia Institute of Hair, Shear Style Barbershop in Painesville, Ohio, opened their doors and welcomed Sunshyne to their team. Sunshyne has cut, dressed, groomed, styled and shaved hundreds of men and boys' hair during her career as a Female Barber.

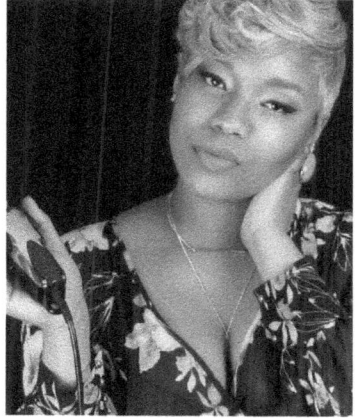

She has fostered a dynamic and socially interactive community at Shear Style Barbershop and work diligently to improve her creative and barbering skills, so that her clients can feel and look better.

Connect with Sunshyne Cannon on Instagram @SunShyne_ TheBarber

NAIL TECHNICIAN

Patricia Patton, also known as Patte is a very passionate, energetic and professional Nail Technician from Cleveland, Ohio. Her motto is "Do What You Want When Ya Poppin." Possessing a keen eye for detail, precision, and having a vibrant personality has helped build a reputation of excellence throughout Ohio.

Patte' received her Bachelor of Arts Degree in Business Management from Notre Dame College of Ohio in 2016. Soon after she received her degree, she followed her dreams to empower people within the beauty industry. She strives to create a memorable experience one client at a time. Patte's clients leave more confident and more knowledgeable about their nails and skin. Her audience is not limited to women, as she accepts children and men.

Patte's goal is to open a local nail academy soon, which will offer daily classes to students interested in enhancing their personal, career and team building skills, as well as those interested in working in the hottest salons in the United States. Patte thrives on continuing to research on the latest products, learn the newest trends and techniques to be able to provide the best and unique designs for her clients and students.

Email: nailsbypatte@gmail.com
Instagram: @Nailsbypatte

CLOTHING LINE OWNER

Dream, manifest and inspire!

Are you dressed to travel Global Kings Global Queens?

Your destination clothing line owner, Gerrell Jones.

Connect with Gerrell on Instagram @ globalkingsglobalqueens

REFERENCES

Sultan A. Latif & Naimah Latif, Slavey: The African American Psychic Trauma page 20, 21